More Brilliant Stories for Assemblies

Elizabeth Sach

Brilliant
PUBLICATIONS

We hope you and your pupils will enjoy the stories in this book. Brilliant Publications publishes many other books for primary school teachers, a few of which are listed below. You may find more details on our website: www.brilliantpublications.co.uk.

Brilliant Stories for Assemblies	978-1-903853-98-6
Positively Me!	978-1-905780-72-3
Smiling Inside, Smiling Outside!	978-1-903853-73-3
Into the Garden of Dreams	978-1-903853-37-5
43 Team-building Activities for Key Stage 1	978-1-903853-81-8
43 Team-building Activities for Key Stage 2	978-1-903853-02-3

Published by Brilliant Publications
Unit 10
Sparrow Hall Farm
Edlesborough
Dunstable
Bedfordshire
LU6 2ES, UK

Tel: 01525 222292
E-mail: info@brilliantpublications.co.uk
Website: www.brilliantpublications.co.uk

The name Brilliant Publications and the logo are registered trademarks.

Written by Elizabeth Sach
Illustrated by Q2A Media
Cover illustration by Catherine Ward
Designed by Q2A Media
Front cover designed by Brilliant Publications

© Text Elizabeth Sach 2010
© Design Brilliant Publications 2010

Printed Book ISBN 978-1-905780-74-7
E-book ISBN 978-0-85747-129-1

First printed and published in the UK in 2010

Introduction

Stories are a powerful and immediate way of conveying emotions, situations and information.

The stories in this book allow the teller to read, refine or adapt a variety of tales for a particular situation or audience. The collection covers a wide range of themes. Different stories can be used at specific times of the year, when issues arise, or just when you are suddenly called upon to do an assembly! Many of them can also be adapted for class assemblies or different key stages.

The assembly stories in this book have been organized according to the themes used in the Department for Education's Social and Emotional Aspects of Learning (SEAL) document:

❖ Changes
❖ New Beginnings
❖ Say No to Bullying
❖ Problem Solving
❖ Going for Goals
❖ Relationships
❖ Getting on and Falling out
❖ Be the Best you Can be
❖ Good to be Me

In addtion, there are some assembly stories linked to the curriculum:

❖ Other religions
❖ Humanities
❖ Science

Many of the stories can be used in connection with more than one SEAL theme, and links to other SEAL themes are indicated on the contents pages (pages 4–5).

Each story ends with suggested questions to explore with the audience. These can be refined into prayers.

	Page	New Beginnings	Getting on and Falling out	Problem Solving	Good to be Me	Going for Goals	Relationships	Be the Best you Can be	Say No to Bullying	Changes	Planning Targets	Celebrating Differences
Changes												
Jacob's Bunny – Bert	6							✔		✔	✔	
Peter the See-through Prawn	9						✔	✔		✔		
Miles of Smiles	12						✔			✔		
The Fire Engine Came to School Today	15				✔					✔		
New Beginnings												
Myra	18	✔		✔			✔					
Once Upon a Time	21	✔			✔						✔	
My Mate Libby's Got Chickens	24	✔								✔		
Say No to Bullying												
The Witness	27						✔		✔			
Problem Solving												
And We Shall Have Snow	30		✔	✔								
Free Choice Time	33			✔	✔	✔						
Jazz Hands	35			✔			✔			✔		
King Nincompoop Goes Green	37			✔			✔	✔				
Spare a Thought for the Teachers	40			✔	✔							✔
Going for Goals												
Football Crazy	43			✔		✔		✔				
Maisie and Sacha	46			✔	✔	✔						
Mario is on Report	49	✔		✔		✔				✔		
The Green Man	52	✔			✔	✔						
Relationships												
Red the Black Labrador	55						✔					✔
What if?	58					✔	✔				✔	
Abigail's Report	61	✔		✔			✔					
Grandma Pitchford's Birthday	64				✔		✔				✔	
The Team Rolls Out Time	67	✔					✔			✔		
Getting on and Falling out												
Daisies are our Silver	70		✔			✔		✔				
I Want! Won't Get	73		✔				✔					
Ratty and Rabbit (AKA Stop and Think)	76		✔			✔		✔				
'Samstan' – The Two-headed Monster	79		✔	✔			✔					
The Eagle and the Lion	82		✔	✔			✔		✔			

	Page	New Beginnings	Getting on and falling out	Problem Solving	Good to be Me	Going for Goals	Relationships	Be the Best you Can be	Say No to Bullying	Changes	Planning Targets	Celebrating Differences
Getting on and Falling out												
The Little Frog and the Owl (AKA: Have you Met my Friend?)	85		✔				✔					
Be the Best you Can be												
Fire in the Forest	88			✔	✔			✔				
Mrs Fuss the Dinner Lady	90			✔	✔			✔				
Spot, Splodge and Smudge (AKA Someone is Telling me Lies)	93	✔		✔				✔				
Good to be Me												
Daphne and Ollie	96		✔		✔		✔					
Jeb the Giant	99			✔	✔		✔					
What's in a Name?	102	✔			✔			✔				
Chip Fat on your Ballet Shoes	105				✔	✔						✔
If Only I were Superman	108			✔	✔		✔					✔
Please Listen	110			✔	✔			✔				
Religions												
Daniel and Koshi	113		✔	✔						✔		
Nisha and the Hare's Fairy	116			✔				✔				
The Tigress and the Dragon	119	✔		✔						✔		
Hanukkah Games	121				✔			✔				
Fishing for Tiddlers	124	✔			✔		✔					
Salematu's Secret Box	127		✔					✔				
We Three Kings	130			✔			✔					
Shanaz Takes the Veil	133	✔		✔			✔			✔		
Humanities												
Evacuation	136			✔				✔				
Who's to Blame?	139							✔	✔			
Wanted - A Friend	142	✔		✔						✔		
Science												
Orange Smarties	144		✔				✔					
The Purple Pansy	147	✔			✔					✔		
Mum Knows Best	149				✔		✔					
The Sunflower Seed	152			✔	✔		✔					
Tell no Lies	155	✔					✔					

Jacob's Bunny – Bert

Theme: Jacob is facing his first day at Nursery School without his mum and he is really worried, and he doesn't understand the feelings going on in his head and tummy! Bert, his ever-present Bunny, comes to the rescue and all is well.

Setting: Nursery and Home

SEAL reference: Changes

Bert was not a typical soft toy Bunny. He had long floppy ears and the widest of smiles. His eyes were deep dark brown and his fur was soft, soft, soft. He was, in fact, six inches of adorable hug.

Jacob hadn't known, when he was born three years ago on November 20th at 10:20 pm, that he already 'owned' Bert.

But he knew it now. He knew that Bert was with him for always.

Right from being a tiny baby, Jacob had cuddled and cuddled him. When sucking his thumb, Jacob had never let go of Bert's ears, and he had even been sick on him! Thankfully, Bert enjoyed being washed by Jacob's Mummy and he usually dried off a treat.

Over the years, Bert had been lost and found many times. Sometimes just a little bit lost and once, *really* lost, for one whole morning!

Bert looked a bit worn and scruffy now. He was a little bald on his ears, but he still had the widest smile that you could ever imagine and, if you looked at him, you couldn't help but smile back.

Today Jacob looked at Bert. 'Do you remember that day when we hid at the back of Grandpa Heath's shed?' he asked him. 'No one could find us at all, until I got the hiccoughs and gave the game away.'

Jacob laughed. 'And what about the time I left you in the men's shoe department at Marks and Spencer's? Grandma and Mummy searched high and low and there you were still sitting inside a black lace-up shoe, size 11!'

Jacob picked Bert up and stuffed him into one of his own shoes as if to remind him of the escapade. 'Grandma said we were lucky that you hadn't slipped down inside and been taken home by a man with *big* feet!'

Bert twitched his ears. Jacob was never sure if he did it himself or whether the draught from the door blew on him and made his ears move. But he always seemed to do a twitch at the right moment.

'I know!' Jacob said, in reply to the twitch. 'You always remember *that* one as well. Grandad Price calls it The Great Escape or The Day Bert the Bunny Did a Runner.'

Jacob picked Bert up again and held him tightly.

'Hardly a run though, Bert, more a roll. You fell out of my hands and rolled all the way down to the bottom of the stand, when we were at a football match. Dad looked everywhere and we thought that it would be the last time we would ever see you. How could we find you among all those feet? Then, just as we gave up hope and started for home, there you were sitting on the turnstile, waiting for us. Some kind person must have seen you and realized that you were pretty special to someone else.'

Jacob looked worried and hugged Bert even tighter. He wondered what would happen to Bert now. Tomorrow would be Jacob's first day at Nursery School. He knew it would be really good fun and that all the Mummies could stay too. *But* the day after that would be Jacob's first day at Nursery on his own.

He knew all his friends would still be there, but he still felt worried and he *still* had butterflies in his tummy.

The next morning when Mummy came to help him put his coat on, she noticed that he was looking a bit glum. 'Are you alright?' she asked him.

Jacob mumbled his answer, a sure sign that he wasn't.

'Come on now,' said Mummy, in her happy voice. 'You can tell me and then we can sort it out together!'

Jacob said nothing, so Mummy decided to battle on with his coat without saying anything else. She didn't want to upset him by asking any more questions. She was sure that once they were at Nursery, and he saw all his friends, Jacob would be fine.

And she was right. Of course!

Jacob and his friends had a great day, especially when they were allowed to play outside on the wheelie toys.

Suddenly it was time to start tidying up, ready to go home. Mrs Nooney called all the new children and their mummies to the 'Sitting Quietly' area. Then in a big voice, she said, 'Now children, you all know that tomorrow your mummies will go home after they have seen you safely inside and they will collect you again later at lunch-time.'

Jacob's tummy lurched. He had forgotten about his worry! He had been having so much fun with his friends. Now it came back, even bigger than before.

Mrs Nooney continued, 'We all know that the first day without Mummy can be tough, so I want you all to bring your favourite soft toy with you tomorrow. Then if you feel you want a big hug, you will have someone here who is good-for-a-hug!,' She pointed to some low-down shelves, near the beanbags. 'All your soft-toys will sit on these shelves tomorrow and watch you having fun, like you have done today. But just in case you need a hug and a little 'time-out', you can always go to snuggle down on a beanbag with your own special toy.'

She smiled encouragingly at all the new children and their mummies.

'Then,' she added, 'when you're ready to go back and play, simply put your toy safely back on the shelf and join in again.'

Everyone seemed to smile at once, it was as if the Sun had slid out from behind a cloud.

Jacob took his mummy's hand and squeezed it. She looked down at him and saw a bright smile shining on his face. It was a smile the size of… well… the size of Bert the Bunny's! She knew exactly why he had been sad that morning. She smiled back and gave his hand a tiny squeeze too.

They understood each other perfectly.

They both realized that there would still be plenty of adventures for Jacob and Bert to enjoy together for a long time yet.

Follow-up questions

- Why do you think Bert the Bunny was so special to Jacob?

- What special things can we do to help us when we are worried?

Peter the See-through Prawn

Theme: Peter does not feel very good about his pale blue colouration. He can't wait to be grown up and opalescent blue like his dad, so he takes matters into his own hands with disastrous effect.

Setting: In a freshwater loch where Peter lives

SEAL reference: Changes

Peter the Prawn hated being see-through blue. In fact, what he hated even more was that he was not just blue, he was baby blue!

His Dad was a rich opalescent blue and he had often told Peter that he only had to wait and he would become as shiny as a pearl too. But Peter could *not* wait!.

It's just silly for a boy prawn to be pale blue, he thought. I'm sure my friends don't like me half as much when I'm so pale.

He didn't mind being small.

He didn't mind having really skinny legs.

He didn't even mind having ridiculously long wavy antennae that got trapped in the oddest of places. No, what he really really did dislike was being this wishy-washy, palest of baby *blue*.

He would rather be any other colour, he decided – even the greenish-brown of the lurid mud at the bottom of the loch – anything – just as long as he wasn't pale blue any more.

So Peter the Prawn decided to do something about it. That's what his dad had advised him to do when he had a problem. Do something about it.

'If you only get 8 out of 10 for your spellings, then it's your problem, Son,' he had said. 'Only you can do something about it, I can't learn them for you. What can you change that will help you to get those two extra marks?'

Peter soon found the answer to the spelling problem. He quickly realized that he always learned his spellings from top to bottom and, by the time he got to numbers eight, nine and ten, he was tired and fed up. So the next week he changed things around and learned them bottom to top for three days and then from top to bottom for the next three days. Then, guess what! He actually got them all correct.

Having learned that lesson, Peter decided that only *he* could find an answer to the problem of his colour. So carefully he made a plan and, the very next day, he set to work.

First he spent his time looking for things that were muddy, weedy and *definitely* dirty.

The bottom of the loch was perfect, he thought. It was covered in soft brown silt that was just the right colour for Peter. He dug down deeply. Soon all his body was wrapped in the loch mud. (Though he did, at least, leave his head and eyes out above the silt, which was quite sensible for a little prawn like him.)

As he stayed there, buried in the mud, he watched the other loch-kids out in the loch. Some were swimming against the current, then whooping and screaming on the free ride back. What fun! Others were gathering loch weed and building dens to see which one would last longest. Finally they all played the game of 'Let's annoy the General'. This was Peter's favourite game.

'The General' was an ancient crab who had lived longer than anyone else the Loch-Kids knew. He had never been caught by a fisherman, never lost a claw in a scrap and he was the grumpiest creature in the whole wide loch. The youngsters loved to tease him.

Peter began to feel left out and lonely. He wondered if the mud had worked its magic yet. 'Best wait,' he decided. 'I want to be sure of a good result.'

Not long afterwards, Peter started to doze. So he was very surprised when a loud voice shouted in his ear, 'What hoh! Peter the Prawn! Who buried you! Been naughty have we?'

Peter nearly jumped out of his skin. He was completely surrounded by a group of mixed Crustaceans, all lads who had hard outside shells and who thought that made them tough.

'Ah! Oh no! No,' stuttered Peter, 'I was a little bit… erm… hot so I decided to cool down in the mud.'

The Crustaceans laughed. It was obvious that Peter was making it up. They pointed their claws at Peter and shouted to others to come and laugh too.

Well, it's now or never, thought Peter. He was sure he must have changed colour by now.

So, with a super-prawn effort, he hauled himself out of the cold, sticky, slimy mud. Momentarily, just enough of the mud and slime stuck to his body… it made him look like a ferocious, pre-historic monster that was rising up from the deep!

The Crustaceans howled in terror and swam away to hide. Peter giggled. He was secretly pleased. He obviously looked really tough now. He walked along the loch-bed, trying to swagger like 'The General'.

The terrible thing now, though, was that *everyone*, he met, ran away from him too. This was not what he had wanted at all. He had simply not wanted to be teased about his colour any more.

All alone, Peter sank to the bottom of the loch. He was too sad to care that the current was very strong there and washing him home. He also didn't realize that the water was washing away all the sticky, slimy mud – even pulling off the weeds and kelp that had been caught in his joints.

Within minutes he was home. 'Hello, Peter the Prawn!' called his mum.

Peter jumped in surprise. Then he looked at his legs – they were pale blue! He checked his body and antennae – they were pale blue too. It hadn't worked! He was still the same colour as always. He was still Peter the Prawn!

'Hurrah!' he cried, dancing around, repeating again and again, 'It didn't work! It didn't work!'

'What didn't work, Peter?' asked his mum.

'Oh, hello, Mum,' said Peter, stalling for time. 'Erm… I decided to change something today, like I did with my spellings, but this one didn't work.'

'Never mind, sweetheart,' said his mum, giving him a big hug, 'some things just can't be changed. We have to work on those things we can change and accept those we can't.'

'Hmm,' thought Peter, 'I wish I'd known that this morning, I wouldn't have spent so long worrying about something that I couldn't change. But, at least, now I know that my *real friends* like me better when I am pale blue and friendly – and not when I'm muddy and tough.'

Follow-up questions

- Why do you think Peter the Prawn hated his colour?

- How important is our outward appearance with regard to how others see us?

- What characteristics do you have that make you special?

Miles of Smiles

Theme: Jonathan is unhappy about the prospect of moving house and it all comes to a head when he realizes that it is all going to happen this week. The school day proves awful and it gets much worse as Mum and the Head arrive in the classroom.

Setting: Moving to a new home

SEAL reference: Changes

Jonathan was worried. His mum and dad had just told him they were going to live in a new place. They had sounded really pleased and excited.

'We've got a beautiful house out in the country,' said Dad.

'We'll be able to go for walks by the river,' said Mum.

At first their cheerfulness had rubbed off on Jonathan. He had smiled and nodded as they explained all about dad's new job. But that night in bed, Jonathan's tummy felt as if it were full of heavy rocks. He couldn't fall asleep, even though he was hugging his toy monkey so very, very tightly.

The next morning was even worse. Just as he was about to enter the playground, his mum said, brightly. 'In you go, Jonathan. I'll be back at break time to tell Mr Street that you will be leaving on Friday. Don't worry, I'll explain all about Dad's new job. Shall I bring in a playtime treat for all the class as a little farewell surprise?'

Without another word, she kissed Jonathan on the head and waved Goodbye. But Jonathan didn't notice. 'Friday?' he repeated.

The blood in his body thundered through his ears, his heart started racing in his chest, his legs felt wobbly and he realized that he was going to cry. He looked round for his mum... but she had gone.

Jonathan curled himself up in the smallest ball he could against the wall. Tears trickled down his cheeks. 'Why did he have to go away from school? He loved it here. Why did his mum and dad want to move so quickly? Why did Dad want a new job anyway?' Jonathan had so many questions.

'Do you want to play?' his friend Tommy asked him softly.

But Jonathan was still in a world of his own. It was another question and he couldn't even manage a reply. He stayed where he was until the school bell rang. Oh, it was such a bad day! And it didn't get any better when he went indoors.

First he spilt water all over the painting that he had been working on for days. Then he refused to get a book, when asked to join the reading group. Mrs Stimpson told him to read on his own in the reading corner.

Finally, just before break time, he felt so bad that he kicked out at the picnic table. He didn't mean to do it, but the table accidentally fell on Molly and hurt her on the arm.

Jonathan pretended that he didn't care – even when Mrs Stimpson knelt down in front of him and explained how naughty he had been. She then asked him firmly to say sorry to Molly.

Suddenly he heard himself shouting at Mrs Stimpson. 'No! I won't say sorry to soppy Molly.' He could see the dismay in Mrs Stimpson's face. He liked his teacher normally, but today he felt as though he hated her.

He looked up and, at that very moment, he saw his mum and Mr Street coming into the classroom. They were looking straight at him. He knew they had heard every word. He saw the sadness on their faces, and he crumpled in a heap on the cold classroom floor.

Almost immediately Mum was there scooping him up and making lovely Mum noises. 'It will all be OK!' she told him. 'We know you're not meaning to be bad. We'll sort it out together. I promise we will,' she told him. 'We'll all make new friends, you, me and Dad.'

Slowly, Jonathan realized that his Mum's voice sounded funny. He sneaked a look at her face – yes, he was right – Mum was crying too!

'You're right, Mum,' he smiled through his tears. He was determined to cheer *her* up now, 'And we'll be much nearer to Grandma and Grandad.' He had suddenly realized that both his mum and dad were finding the move hard too.

'It will be like a great adventure for all of us,' said Mum. 'Dad in his new job and you at your new school, me in our new home.' That made Jonathan think.

He imagined Dad at his first day at work. Poor old Dad! It would be worse than a first day at school. And Dad wouldn't even be able to ask for a hug! This thought made Jonathan laugh. His mum laughed with him, relieved that he seemed to be cheering up at last.

Mum stayed with Jonathan throughout break time, while Mr Street explained about the move to Mrs Stimpson. Afterwards, Mum was invited to join in Circle Time, so that they could share the treat she had bought and tell the other children all about their move.

'And,' said Mrs Stimpson, 'we're going to play our favourite game, Miles of Smiles where everyone gets to tell

the class about something that makes them smile.'

Jonathan smiled a watery smile at his mum. He loved that game too. He hoped they would play it at his new school.

His mum smiled back.

'There you are,' she said, 'one good smile leads to another.'

And Jonathan knew it was true.

Follow-up questions

- Why do you think a worry can sometimes make us bad-tempered?

- Do you think Jonathan was right to think at first that his mum and dad weren't concerned about the move? Why?

- Being positive and happy is contagious – what might you do to help someone who looked sad or lonely?

The Fire Engine Came to School Today

Theme: The Fire Brigade is visiting school today and for most of the class it is a cause for excitement, but for Danny it brings back terrible memories of the fire at his Grandpa's cottage which did a lot of damage.

Setting: School

SEAL reference: Changes

Danny knew all about fire engines. They had warning sirens and large, flashing blue lights. He also knew they made him feel afraid. He knew that fire was bad and hurt people like his Grandpa. He knew that, once the fire was over, you felt poorly for weeks and that your home was gone.

Consequently, Danny was not excited when the teacher at his new school announced 'a treat'. Following Class Two's excellent research on 'The Great Fire of London', a fire engine would be coming to the school next week. Class Two would be able to see exactly how far firefighting had progressed since 1666.

Mr Lee's face beamed as he continued. 'Some of you will be lucky enough to climb on board and press the siren,' he said. 'Others will be able to wear the firefighters' helmets or to look at the breathing apparatus that the firefighters have to wear.'

The children squirmed in anticipation at the fun they would have. All except Danny – his blood ran cold, his hands became sweaty and he felt sick.

Mrs Myers, the Teaching Assistant, noticed Danny turn pale. 'Are you feeling alright, Daniel?' she asked, kindly.

Danny looked up at her, his eyes now full of tears. 'I want my Mummy,' he sobbed.

Mrs Myers stood up and encouraged Danny to go out of the classroom. She smiled across at Mr Lee, who nodded his approval, as he carried on explaining to the rest of the children just how exciting Monday's visit would be.

'Now remember,' he told them, 'tell the firefighters who bring the fire engine everything you can remember about the beginning of an organized fire service. Also – remember there is no rushing about with buckets of water and hooks to tear down the thatch these days – simply dial 999 and ask for the fire service.'

All the children agreed that they would remember and some asked if they could show their artwork to the firefighters. Mr Lee said he would simply choose a few pieces, because he wanted the crew to have lots of time to tell them all about today's fire service.

Once outside with Mrs Myers, Daniel's memories all came flooding back: the fire at Grandpa's cottage; the dark December night!

Danny and his two sisters had travelled to Wales to spend Christmas with Gran and Grandpa. They were all fast asleep, even though a howling wind was raging outside.

Suddenly, Mum had come into their bedroom and woken them up. She was frantic, not like Mum at all, and that made Danny feel very frightened.

'Right, guys!' she had panted. 'Up. Get dressed as quickly as you can. Bring your duvets down for extra warmth. The beam inside Grandpa's chimney is on fire!'

It was bedlam. Mum went off to wake Gran and Grandpa. The children couldn't find their clothes in the dark. Louise, his little sister, began to cry. Dad popped in to help and this made matters even worse.

Soon they were all outside in the snow and wind, waiting for the fire engine to arrive. It didn't come…. And still it didn't come…

Dad and Grandpa kept popping back indoors to check that the fire was still only in the chimney. On their last visit, Grandad decided to check the bedroom above the chimney breast.

At that very moment, there was a huge whoosh of flame that spouted out of the chimney. Mum and Gran began shouting for the two men to come back outside.

Danny saw Grandpa's face in the bedroom window upstairs!

Danny and the girls joined in the shouting.

That's why no one heard the fire engine coming up the hill, until it was nearly at the door. The wailing siren made the whole family almost leap out of their skins.

The next hour was indescribable: noise; cold; Grandpa being carried out of the cottage on a stretcher looking really poorly; everyone nearly choking on the thick black smoke.

Much later, they sat for ages in the warm hospital, waiting for news of Grandpa.

Next morning, Grandpa had to stay in hospital to make sure that he got better. The rest of them went back to the cottage to collect emergency clothes.

The sight that met them was terrible. The Fire Officer explained that they hadn't been able to save the cottage. The wind had fanned the flames and the fire had been so strong that it had spread through the entire building.

So, no! Danny did *not* like fire – or fire engines.

Later that day, Mrs Myers had a word with Mr Lee, who made arrangements. There were some special things that he wanted Danny to learn about fires and how to prevent them.

On the Monday, Danny got a surprise. He was paired with a kind firefighter, who had a little boy of his own the same age as Danny. He took time to explain to

Danny that the old beam which had been left in his grandpa's wall should have been removed when the new fireplace was installed. The wood had become old and dry and this meant that it had caught fire easily, just like the houses in 1666. The firefighter explained that houses were not built like that today.

The firefighter also asked Danny how his Grandpa was feeling now.

Danny told him that following the disaster his gran and grandpa had had nowhere to live. His mum and dad had bought a bigger house, there in the village, so that they could all live together.

'Does that mean you get to see them every day?' asked the firefighter.

'You bet!' answered Danny, looking happy for the first time in ages.

'You see!' exclaimed the firefighter. 'Every cloud has a silver lining.'

Danny smiled. He had learned a lot today. Now he knew not to be afraid, but to be glad. Without the fire service, his Grandpa might not have been rescued from the cottage.

He even thought that one day he might grow up to be a firefighter too. He might even be the hero who saved someone's life!

Follow-up questions

- Do you think that Dad and Grandpa were wise to go back into the house once they had found the fire?

- What is the most important thing to try to *be* and *stay being* when you first hear and respond to a fire alarm?

- Sometimes we forget to be grateful for our happy life. What could we be grateful for?

Myra

Theme: Being a 'carer' when you are still very young is a lonely place to be, but most children do it willingly because of the love they have for the other person. Myra was just such a child and it was one of the seemingly small, insignificant things that suddenly made it all too much, and set her on the road to finding help.

Setting: Looking after Mum who is disabled and at home

SEAL reference: New Beginnings

Myra stirred the teabag around in the cup. She was extra careful with the boiling water today; yesterday she had scalded her hand. She had had to put it under cold running water for ten minutes, which had made her late with her mum's breakfast. Mum had wanted to know why, but Myra hadn't had chance to explain, because she would have been late for school again.

Myra already had five late marks this term and two detentions – any more and there would be a phone call home. Not that Mum could take the call; the telephone was too far from her bed and even if she could have reached it, her speech was now so bad, no one would understand her words. Myra's mum had a painful disease that meant her muscles were getting more and more inefficient. Myra did all she could to help.

Today was Myra's birthday, but there would be no party, no cake, no candles, no friends. Just Myra and her mum – a self-sufficient unit of two. Her mum had been poorly for three years now and she was getting worse and worse. Two years ago her dad had left because he couldn't stand the strain, he said. So there was no one else.

Myra tried not to be sad or angry – she loved being a little housewife and helping her mum. She loved to make the house look tidy. She loved to do the cooking. She had a basic menu she could produce every week, even if it was a bit boring. And if her mum managed a smile, it was reward enough. But Myra did feel lonely and upset sometimes.

Myra heard the letterbox flap. 'Not another bill,' she thought, as she went to collect the post. She was completely unprepared for what she found lying on the mat. There was a bright green envelope, addressed to her. Inside was a garish, cheap card with a girl on the front. She was dressed in lots of 'bling' and 'glitter'.

But it was the short message inside that tore her to pieces.

> Hope you are having a fab day
> Double figures at LAST!
> Your loving Dad x

Straightaway, Myra felt angry and as if her heart were going to break. She was angry with her dad for not knowing what her young life was like. She felt broken-hearted because he thought the last three words could make up for everything. 'Your loving Dad!'

She looked at the picture. She felt guilty, because it wasn't her mum's fault that she was ill. BUT Myra desperately wanted a chance to be like that girl on the front, dressing up and trying on jewellery, or the chance to go into town on Saturday mornings with her friends.

She stuffed the envelope into her pocket. 'Mum's breakfast,' she thought. 'I must take it up. I'm just being stupid.'

She went to the taps and splashed cold water over her face. But the tears came again. This time they wouldn't stop. Try as she might, the floodgates were open.

For the first time ever, Myra left the house without taking Mum her breakfast; without helping her to get out of bed; without dressing her and washing her face; and without combing her hair.

Myra was out of the house, running. Running away from everything… away and as far away as she could go, almost without realising what she was doing!

She didn't stop. She passed the bus station. She passed the new shopping mall. She ran on through the old part of town and past the huge Victorian church. She ran till she was exhausted and out in the fields beyond. There she stopped.

She fell in a crumpled heap and cried – only this time she cried noisily, no keeping it in to protect Mum now. She cried till she was exhausted.

Myra heard the police siren, long before she saw the patrol car. She thought it was chasing someone speeding on the motorway, so she was surprised when it appeared up ahead. She was sitting on the grass verge. The car began to slow down and Myra realized someone was getting out and coming over to her. She sat very still, her eyes as wide as a hooting owl!

It was a policewoman. She looked clean and smart. 'Hello there,' she said standing a little way off. 'Myra, isn't it?' Myra nodded. 'My name's WPC Meadows, funny eh! Out here in the countryside.'

Myra didn't laugh. She just kept on staring.

'Your mum rang us, on 999,' she explained.

'But she can't,' Myra said, simply.

'You'll be surprised what folk can do when they are determined enough,' said WPC Meadows, 'no matter what it costs them.'

Myra looked blank. Her mum must have rolled out of bed and dragged herself to the phone! 'Oh, no!' she gasped.

'It's all right. Your mum's in safe hands now and so are you! Chip off the old block, as they say. You must have got your determination from your mum! How have you managed all these years, Myra, with no one to help?'

Myra felt hot tears streaming down her cheeks again.

'Come on,' said WPC Meadows, gently. 'We'll give you a lift home, shall we?'

Myra nodded and walked with her to the patrol car.

From that day on, nurses and carers came to visit daily to look after Mum and to help with the shopping and the housework. By the end of the month, Myra and her mum had moved into a special flat, with lot of gadgets to help her mum become a little more independent. But best of all Myra joined the Youth Club for 'Children who Care'. There she had met lots of people, all different ages, who could understand why she did all she could for her mum, because they were 'carers' too. They swapped notes about disasters they had suffered and laughed about them.

Weeks later, Myra found the livid green envelope again when she emptied her pockets. 'This was the best thing that ever happened to me and Mum,' she thought. 'Remarkable really!' Her dad had given her the best present ever and he wasn't even aware. 'Maybe I'll get in touch again one day and let him know.'

Follow-up questions

- Why do you think Myra did so much to help her mum without telling anyone?

- What types of things might have helped Myra at the Youth Club she eventually joined?

Once Upon a Time

Theme: Alexis is in her bedroom when she first meets a Shrub, a tiny, tiny person from a race which has never learned the meaning of the words 'to share'. She is astonished and sets about showing this person the joys of sharing.

Setting: Alexis' bedroom

SEAL reference: New Beginnings; Relationships

Once upon a time, so long ago that no one can remember it, the world was full of tiny people. They were of every kind you can imagine: Fairies, Elves, Fauns, Borrowers, Pixies, Wee Folk and so on and so on.

But the kind of people that no one remembers at all were the Shrubs. The Shrubs were extremely small and very shy, which is why memories were so few and why they became a race completely lost to the world of Big Folk.

Do not think that small and shy meant that they were not also clever and adventurous, because they were both in abundance. But there was just one bad thing about Shrubs. Shrubs were not very good at sharing. Maybe it was because they all looked the same. Every Shrub had blue hair, yellow eyes, green coats, red trousers, purple shoes, and they would *never* share anything. Which is why lots and lots of them chose to live on their own with their own possessions, safely hidden away in their own little houses.

Imagine then, one little girl's surprise, when she woke up one day and found a Shrub pulling something off her desk! For a moment she thought it was one of her dolls, but when it moved she quickly realized it was not.

'Hey, who are you?' she called. The Shrub leapt off the desk and scurried behind her slippers.

'I can still see you!' said the little girl. She raised her voice to let the creature know that she wasn't afraid. The tiny Shrub shot behind the wardrobe.

'That's no good,' she giggled. 'You'll get covered in dust and fluff and get the sneezes.'

'Get the what's?' asked the Shrub.

'Sneezes. Come out and I'll tell you all about them.'

She waited and waited, but the Shrub did not appear.

The little girl crept slowly out of bed and along the carpet. She lay on her side and looked under the wardrobe.

Very quietly she said, 'Come on, little creature, I won't hurt you.'

'Promise?' asked the Shrub.

'Cross my heart,' she whispered. She held her breath for fear that she might blow the creature over.

Slowly the tiny rainbow appeared.

'You can't have it back!' he shouted. 'Finders, keepers – losers, weepers!'

'What can't I have back?'

'This table, it's mine now. Finders, keepers.'

'I know, you just said all that.' She tried not to laugh, because he didn't actually have a table. He had a brass drawing pin from her desk – which, she admitted, *was* exactly the right height as a table for him.

'What's your name?' asked the rainbow vision in front of her.

'Alexis,' answered the little girl, politely. 'What's yours?'

'Not telling. Don't share,' replied the Shrub, as if that was perfectly normal.

Now Alexis had been learning about sharing at Playgroup and she knew it was quite hard to do. Sometimes, you simply had to practice. But she knew

it was really nice when someone else shared with you. She wanted to explain all this to the Shrub… but this was just silly, how could they talk if she didn't know his name.

'You need to tell me your name,' she said.

'No!' shouted the bad-tempered little creature.

'That's not fair, I told you mine, if we're to be friends, what shall I call you?'

The Shrub thought for quite a long time before he answered. He didn't have any friends.

He decided that he should be honest with the huge creature that had caught him 'collecting'. He decided to keep 'it' happy and not make 'it' angry.

'You can call me Shrub. We're all Shrubs, but it doesn't matter, 'cos you'll never meet another one. If they find out I've been seen, they will probably make me go and live beyond the deep, dark forest.' And he started to sniffle.

'Oh, please, don't get upset,' said Alexis. 'I won't tell anyone, here or there or anywhere. We can both keep this a secret.' And she tore a tiny corner off a tissue and placed it gently in front of the tiny creature, called Shrub.

He blew his nose and looked up at her, 'Promise?' he asked.

'You bet!' agreed Alexis.

Alexis had decided to be a friend to the creature and to prove that she meant what she said, she added, 'Would you like some chairs to go with your table,

Shrub? I've got too many in my dolls house so you could have three or four if you want.'

'Chairs! Chairzzzz? As in more than one?' he asked in surprise.

'Yes, more than one,' answered Alexis. 'You'll need at least two so that a friend can come for a meal or play a game with you.'

'I don't understand,' said Shrub.

'Life is much more fun when you share what you have with others,' said Alexis. 'You can share sweets, cakes, games, toys.'

'I see,' said the Shrub. He was enjoying being here with this girl who was sharing her stuff with him. He had even begun thinking about what he might bring to share with her from his world.

'You must also learn to take turns if we're to be proper friends,' said Alexis very seriously.

'What's a turn?' asked the Shrub.

Alexis laughed.

'It's alright, Shrub, I'll teach you and then we can be real friends.'

The next time Shrub came to visit Alexis, he brought something with him.

He said it was an umbrella, but in fact it was a Dandelion seed head.

'This is for you,' he said, handing it to Alexis. 'When you let it float in the air, you will see I've put a tiny fragment of Moonbeam in the seed, so it will never be truly dark in your bedroom ever again.'

'It's really beautiful,' breathed Alexis. 'I shall always treasure our first share Shrub.'

'It won't ever fade or go out you know,' said Shrub. 'I spent ages choosing what to bring you this first time.'

'Does that mean we will be sharing other things too?' asked Alexis.

'You bet!' laughed Shrub, echoing Alexis' own words. 'Now I understand sharing, I think it's the best thing I've ever learned. Let's play a game and you can teach me how to take turns.'

Follow-up questions

- What was possibly the most important thing that the Shrub learned about sharing?
- For what sort of games do you need to wait and take turns?

My Mate Libby's Got Chickens

Theme: Errol wants to give his Mum a birthday present that she will really love. The science behind the Modroc is a bit beyond him and his dreams collapse in a heap on the table. Uncle Zeb saves the day and thinks of the perfect present.

Setting: At home, in the garden shed

SEAL reference: New Beginnings

Errol thought long and hard about what he might give his mum for her birthday. She liked flowers, but they died. She liked chocolates, but they were soon eaten – especially when Errol was around! She liked pictures, but he had painted zillions for her, beginning on his first day at Nursery school.

Errol remembered that she had really liked the clay hand-print that he had made in Infants School, before he could even write his own name! It had a sentence underneath that Melanie, the classroom assistant, had written, it said…

'Mothers hold their children's hands for a few years and their hearts for ever.'

Yes, she had really liked it, so much she had cried! How silly was that?

'You were such a little shrimp of a lad, then,' she would sniff. 'Look at you now, you'll soon be taller than me!' Errol was six and a half and only reached up to his Mum's waist, but there again, how daft were Mums?

Nevertheless, this had given Errol an idea. What if he made her another hand.

Not an impression this time, but a model of his very own hands. He would use the Modroc modelling kit that Uncle Zeb had given him for his last birthday and which he hadn't even opened yet.

'I'll show you how to use it properly one day,' Uncle Zeb had promised. But it was Mum's birthday tomorrow and Uncle Zeb was away on tour with his band. There was no chance that he would visit before then.

'Not to worry,' thought Errol, 'how hard can it be?' Errol ran up to his bedroom and got the kit.

'I'm going to play in the shed,' he shouted to his mum as he passed. She was busy working at the computer in the office. 'Call me when dinner is ready.'

'Will do,' said Mum.

Errol carefully set out everything that he needed on the shed table. He looked at the instructions and tried to follow them.

First, he scrunched up some paper and made a model of his hands. Then he put the Modroc in a bucket. He added water and gently stirred the Modroc with a stick. When it was all mixed together and looking good, he began to wrap the strips around the model of his hands. He didn't think it would take too long to set.

When it was dry, he planned to paint the hands and finally to add Mum's favourite nail polish colour to the tips of the fingers. 'That will finish it off nicely,' he said to himself.

But as soon as he started to add the watery paint to cover his model, it all went wrong. Soon his beautiful idea was lumped on the table in a soggy heap. It looked like a melted jelly mixed with trifle.

At that moment, he felt a hand on his shoulder. He didn't dare look up in case it was Mum. He knew he was spattered with Modroc paste and peachy coloured paint, and that the shed was a mess.

'What were you trying to do, Kid?' came a voice. It was Uncle Zeb!

At once Errol burst into tears. He had been trying to make his Mum the best present ever. He had planned it carefully. He had read the instructions. He had done the best he could, but it was a disaster.

His eyes told Uncle Zeb the whole story. Uncle Zeb had always understood Errol. He remembered what he had been like when he was a little boy, whenever he looked at his nephew.

'Birthday?' asked Uncle Zeb.

Errol nodded.

'Don't worry, we'll think of something,' said Uncle Zeb. 'But first we'd better clear up this mess, before your mum comes asking questions.' Uncle Zeb took off his leather jacket, and they set to work together.

'My mate Libby's got chickens.' Uncle Zeb suddenly announced, out of the blue.

Errol gave him a long look.

'They lay pale blue and lilac-coloured eggs, as well as really dark brown ones and, of course, all the usual shades,' he added.

Errol still looked mystified.

'We could nip up to her house,' he pointed ahead. 'We could choose a special half a dozen for your mum's birthday.' He sounded excited.

'Eggs!' laughed Errol.

'Yeah man! New beginnings, don't you see. Deep, dark yellow yolks, free range, lovely flavour, your mum will love them!'

Errol knew Uncle Zeb was right. He always was. Errol smiled and nodded almost too tired to speak. Suddenly he had a thought.

'How did you get here? Weren't you away with the band?'

'Slipped back, just to wish my big sister Happy Birthday.' He grinned at Errol. 'As your Gran used to say: always do the best you can – never mind the cost in time or effort. That way folk will know that you really care.'

Uncle Zeb was talking to a tired boy: but he knew that Errol understood. This was exactly what Errol had been doing, when Zeb had found him – trying his best.

'Come on, Kid,' said Uncle Zeb, picking up his jacket. 'We better get off to find those chickens before it's time for them to go to bed… *and* before your mum finishes cooking dinner and starts asking questions!'

Follow-up questions

- Why did Errol want to give his mum something extra special for her birthday?

- What was the most helpful thing that Uncle Zeb did or said for Errol?

The Witness

Theme: Ranpresh is terrified of 'The Gang' and gets attacked on the way home from school. Hannah is a witness but she is afraid to do anything about it. At last she finds the courage to be part of the solution rather than being part of the problem.

Setting: School

SEAL reference: Say No to Bullying

Ranpresh sat at the back of the classroom watching… listening… Was this the day that he would really find out why the 'bullies' in Class 5 always picked on him.

He didn't hold out much hope. He had been here so many times before. He could probably write a book on how many times he had been bullied, there were so many! The only problem was that there seemed no way out, at least not for him.

He risked a sneaky look at the leader of 'The Gang'.

Harjeet!

Ranpresh was so scared of him that he had to breathe deeply even before he dare turn his head towards him. When he did, Harjeet was looking straight back at him!

Ranpresh's hands were sweaty and his heart began to thump. Harjeet had a vile sly grin on his face.

'He knows I'm scared,' thought Ranpresh. He knows and he is enjoying it.

Fear now ran through Ranpresh's whole body, even though he knew he was safe in the classroom. He tried to breathe slowly and deeply as his Uncle had taught him when he had come face-to-face with his first snake, during a family visit to India. It didn't help.

Harjeet, meanwhile, knew exactly what he was doing. He knew that he had pushed Ranpresh into being so frightened of 'The Gang' that now they didn't even have to hurt him. The occasional threat: 'to watch himself on the way home' or 'tomorrow might be the day!' was enough to reduce Ranpresh to a trembling wreck.

Harjeet sat back in his chair. 'Easy!' he thought.

He was grinning to himself now because he knew that Ranpresh was trapped. He was suffering the same fear and helplessness now as if they had actually 'cornered' him, which Harjeet still planned to do anyway.

Ranpresh's chest was tight. He felt as though he was suffocating. His face was burning, but his hands and feet were like blocks of ice.

'Ranpresh? Ranpresh… can you hear me. Are you alright?' asked Miss Howard.

Ranpresh tried to speak, but his mouth was dry. He tried to smile, but his lips wobbled. He was trying not to cry.

He managed a feeble wave to imply that he was OK – just before everything went black and he fell to the floor.

The class was in uproar, girls shrieking, boys giggling. They thought it was all a great joke. Then the bell rang for afternoon break.

'Class 5!' shouted Miss Howard over the noise. 'Out to play, please!' She knelt down by Ranpresh.

Ranpresh tried to get up, but Miss Howard made him stay where he was.

Ranpresh did as he was told, he felt too groggy to do anything else. He also felt silly now and he realized there would be questions to answer both here and at home. But he knew he couldn't tell anyone the truth about 'The Gang'!

Miss Howard told Ranpresh to spend the last lesson in Mrs Hague's room. This was a quiet place where you could say what you really felt and no one misunderstood or overreacted. Consequently, when it came to home-time, he was feeling quite calm. He might even get a few days off school as a result of his fainting.

The school secretary arrived, just before the Bell, with a message.

'Ranpresh, your mum's been in touch. She has to work late today, so your Grandad is going to pick you up. Your mum says you are to start walking to save your Grandad's legs.' And with that she turned on her heel and rushed off with her next message.

Mrs Hague watched all the colour drain from Ranpresh's face. He sank back into his chair as if all the wind had been sucked out of him.

'Are you feeling poorly again, Ranpresh. You've gone a funny colour. Can I do anything.'

'No,' moaned Ranpresh on a whisper of breath. 'No, thank you, Mrs Hague.'

'I'll go and get your coat and your book bag for you and I'll walk you to the gate, maybe your Grandad will be there by then,' she said.

At the gate, there was no sign of Grandad, so Mrs Hague said, 'Goodbye' to Ranpresh.

He buttoned up his coat and tied all his books and bags around him. He hoped they might protect him from the onslaught he was expecting. Then, all his preparations made, he decided to run like the wind for as long and as far as he could. Maybe he would get to Grandad before the bullies got to him!

Ranpresh wasn't two minutes from the school gate when they pounced!

Hannah saw everything from her bedroom window. She was horrified, but felt she was too far away to help. She was also too afraid to get involved.

So, next morning, she had a terrible shock in Assembly. The Headteacher announced that Ranpresh was in hospital. He was very poorly and he said they should all think of him in a time of quiet.

He also added that if anyone had seen or hcard anything of the incident last night they should tell him straight after the Assembly.

Hannah was worried. What should she do? Then she remembered what Mrs Hague had often told them. 'If you can't decide what to do, check how you feel inside. If it feels bad; it *is* bad. So tell someone!'

Hannah looked inside herself. She knew why Ranpresh had fainted yesterday. She knew about 'The Gang' – all the children did. She knew that bullies rely on everyone's fear to keep them out of trouble.

'But not any more!' thought Hannah. She was suddenly very angry. She had heard them boasting at the school gate that morning about what they had done and how 'safe' they felt.

Hannah found herself walking, no, not walking, storming towards the

Headteacher's office. Outside the Head's door, she didn't hesitate. She gave three loud knocks, waited for a moment, and pushed open the door.

'Why, hello Hannah…' The Headmaster didn't get any further. Hannah's torrent of anger filled the room.

Then there was a pausc bcfore Hannah looked the Head straight in the eye… 'And,' she added, 'I don't mind who knows it was me who told you, 'cos I'm not scared of them anymore.'

A few days later she saw Mrs Hague in the corridor. She smiled and gave Hannah the 'Thumbs Up' sign and a big grin. She pointed to the display where she had put up a huge banner that read.

'IF YOU ARE NOT PART OF THE SOLUTION; YOU ARE PART OF THE PROBLEM!'

Hannah gave Mrs Hague a 'high-five' and walked on smiling. She knew which half she was in.

Follow-up questions

- Why is it often so hard to say if you are being bullied?
- What gave Hannah the courage to tell about what she had seen?
- Bullies rely on three things: your fear, your silence and the imbalance of power. Remember, always 'Tell, tell, tell!'

And We Shall Have Snow

Theme: Poor Robin has a problem and he is feeling very angry, even little Blue Tit seems unable to help him, until Robin sees the error of his ways, when it is almost too late.

Setting: The farmyard

SEAL reference: Problem Solving

*The north wind doth blow, and we shall have snow
and what will poor Robin do then?
Poor thing.
He'll sit in the barn
to keep himself warm.
And hide his head under his wing.
Poor thing.*

Little Robin puffed out all his feathers, 'til he looked like a completely round ball of brown and red fluff, with two ridiculous twig-like legs sticking out of the bottom.

He had never heard the poem, but he knew exactly what it felt like.

Robin was cold and hungry. He was cold, because no matter how much he tried to trap warm air between his feathers, the icy blast from the East cut through to freeze his tiny frame. He was also hungry, because no matter how hard he tried to hover over the food table, like other birds did, or hang using his delicate feet, like the Blue Tit, someone always knocked him off balance and he fell to the ground like a small bomb, causing a tiny puff of snowflakes to billow up.

'It isn't fair!' thought Robin. 'I'm a ground feeder, not an aerial-acrobat. Why don't the humans put *my* food down on the ground for me to peck at easily?'

He stood behind a fence post, hiding from the wind and feeling miserable.

A tiny Blue Tit came hurtling towards him, blown by the force of the Winter gale.

'Wheee! Oops, sorry!' he chirruped to Robin, as he landed on his feet.

'Watch out!' twittered Robin angrily. 'What do you think you are doing?'

The tiny Blue Tit shivered and tried valiantly to stay upright on his feet.

'I can't get a grip!' he shouted over the storm. 'Isn't this fun, Robin?'

'No!' yelled Robin, over the howling wind. 'I can't get any food!'

'Oh dear, that's awful, can I help in any way?'

'I don't think so,' said Robin testily – as if a tiny Blue Tit could help a Robin nearly twice his own size.

'Why don't you go to the feeding station that the humans have put out for us?' asked the cheery, little bird.

Robin felt like squashing him. 'It's alright for you lot,' he moaned, 'they put all the food in the correct places for you! They don't remember that I can't hang on and eat the fat-balls or the peanuts. I have long toes and need to stand on something to eat my food!'

Blue Tit tried again.

'I know what!' he tweeted. 'I'll go and feed and as I do I will drop some bits onto the ground and then you can eat them all up!'

'Oh, for goodness sake!' stamped Robin. (Blue Tit noticed his legs were very long and spindly and that his toes looked even longer!) '*Then*,' Robin sulked. 'I will have to compete with the Sparrows and the Blackbirds. Have you seen the size of those Blackbirds!'

Blue Tit thought hard. He wasn't one to give up easily, even in the face of such stiff opposition.

'I've got it!' he screeched, over the driving wind and snow. 'Why don't you fly up to the Big House, where the humans live, and sit on their window-sill looking all forlorn and hungry. You could even tap on the glass with your beak. Maybe the humans will notice you and come to your rescue. It has worked for me.'

Robin gave Blue Tit a scornful look. He spent enough time with humans in the Summer, eating all the worms and insects in their gardens.

'You could just give it a try,' said the little bird, feeling that he was fast running out of options to help. 'It might work, jog their memories, you know?'

'I'm not sure,' said Robin, still feeling sorry for himself. 'I admit I do look really pretty against the snow with my bright red breast. They even have special cards made at Christmas with my portrait on to decorate their houses. So why do they forget me in the Winter, when there is so little food and I most need their help? It's not fair!'

But Blue Tit didn't reply. Poor Blue Tit had been blown away by the ferocious East wind.

'Typical,' Robin thought, 'no one cares about me. I'll just hide in the barn and keep myself warm and hide my head under my wing! Poor me!'

Blue Tit had landed in the lee of the garden shed, where the wind could not blow. He decided to have a rest, catch his breath, then make one last push to get back to his nest before he froze to death. The time spent with Robin had cost him dearly.

'Some birds just cannot be helped,' he thought. 'They are so full of self pity, they imagine they are the only ones with a problem.' His eyes began to close, he was very tired, after battling with the weather for so long. It would be very dangerous for him if he fell asleep.

Robin, meanwhile, was trying to find a good spot in the Barn – when out of the corner of his little black eye, he noticed a tiny ball of fluff behind the garden shed. He couldn't be sure, but he thought it was Blue Tit!

Suddenly he forgot all his worries, plunged down to the barn floor and flew low over the snow to the tiny bird.

'Blue Tit! Blue Tit, wake up! You must *not* fall asleep. You will surely freeze to death and never wake up again.'

Blue Tit didn't respond.

Robin was terrified. This little bird had spent so long trying to cheer *him* up and be helpful, that he had probably used up all his energy and warmth and was now too tired to make it home.

Robin snuggled up close to the tiny frame of Blue Tit. He fluffed up his feathers to make extra warmth.

'Come on, Little Chap,' he twittered softly. 'Come on. Wake up.'

It took quite a long time, but eventually Robin felt BlueTit's heart beating more strongly. Then he felt his tiny wings begin to flutter.

'Oh! Thank goodness, you are alive!' Robin greeted him.

'Only thanks to you, my friend,' he whispered. 'You could have gone to sleep in your nice warm barn and… Oh, I don't want to think about what might have happened.'

'No problem,' sang Robin and for the first time that day he felt happy. 'One good turn deserves another. Now off you fly home, before you get chilled again.'

As he flew away, Robin clearly heard Blue Tit call, 'Don't forget the window trick.'

Twenty minutes later, Robin was eating mealy worms and insect mix for all he was worth. BlueTit's ruse had worked. The humans had spotted Robin straight away and remembered how much they loved him!

Follow-up questions

- Why, do you think, did Robin spend so much time complaining and doing nothing to help himself?
- Do you agree that 'one good turn deserves another'?

Free Choice Time

Theme: Tizzy and Kezia are the very best of friends, until the fateful day when they are allowed to choose for themselves what they would like to do. In the end, the girls discover that they can be different and still be friends.

Setting: First school

SEAL reference: Problem Solving

Tizzy and Kezia were best of friends, just like their mummies. They were full of life and always laughing – happy as could be. They didn't really need any anyone else, because they always had each other.

Although they were only five years old, they had already been on holiday together, joined dance classes together, had birthday parties together, you name it, they had probably done it – together.

When they started school everyone was worried they might be in different classes, but no, they were even put in the same class – together!

At the end of week one, the teacher explained to the children all about 'Free Choice' time. This meant that on Friday afternoons, when all the class were quite weary, Mrs Dumbarton would set out all the different areas with separate activities. The children could then choose to do one, or all of them, as they wished.

Tizzy and Kezzie, as Kezia quickly became known, were excited.

When Mrs Dumbarton opened the classroom door, they both immediately saw what they wanted to do. Tizzy headed straight for the table full of paper, in all shapes and sizes, with crayons and paints and coloured pens of every hue.

She settled herself down in the chair near the window and began to 'colour in'. She was contented and started to really enjoy herself. But at that moment, Kezzie came over to the table.

'Come on,' she said, pulling Tizzy's jumper. 'Come and work with me at the Science table – it's got lots of water and floaters and sinkers – it's great fun.'

'Uh, huh?' murmured Tizzy, deeply engrossed in her picture.

33

'No! Come and play with me,' whined Kezzie, and she pulled Tizzy's jumper again. But this time, she did it harder and this made Tizzy's arm drag her crayon straight across her colouring. This made Tizzy cross with Kezzie and she pushed her away.

Kezzie lost her balance and fell back against a low table and hurt her arm. She began to cry. At once this made Tizzy afraid and sad all at once, she leaped up from her chair and went to comfort her friend. She wondered if Mrs Dumbarton would be angry with her. She had only wanted to do colouring during Free Choice time.

'She pushed me!' wailed Kezzie. 'She pushed me hard!'

'Oh, Tizzy,' said Mrs Dumbarton. She sounded disappointed and cross. 'What have you done?'

Tizzy was unsure and confused. It was Kezzie who'd spoilt *Tizzy's* picture, she was the naughty one. But no one was asking *her* what had happened. So she too began to cry too.

'That won't help you,v said Mrs Dumbarton. 'I think you owe Kezia a big apology, don't you?'

'No,' answered Tizzy, truthfully. She was still unsure why everyone thought she was the naughty girl.

'Oh, Tizzy!' grumbled Mrs Dumbarton.

'I want my mummy,' cried Tizzy.

'Your mummy won't be pleased with what you have done,' said Mrs Dumbarton.

Now Tizzy was even more confused, why would Mummy not be pleased with her. She had been colouring a beautiful picture for her to stick on the fridge, except Kezia had spoilt it, because she wanted Tizzy to do the same as her. She always did!

What a pickle both girls were in.

Not long afterwards, both mummies arrived. They spent time talking to the girls and Mrs Dumbarton and soon they got to the bottom of the problem. It was sort of alright between the girls by the time they went home, but it was difficult for either of them to feel good about each other.

Mrs Dumbarton said, 'Forgive and forget.'

The mummies said, 'It's over now, so not to worry.'

But Tizzy and Kezzie knew deep down that something had changed. They had both learned a hard lesson in thinking about how others feel and not just wanting your own way all the time.

They were still best friends; just a little wiser.

Follow-up questions

- Do you think Tizzy was right to be cross with Kezzie?
- Was Mrs Dumbarton right to ask the girls to 'forgive and forget'?

Jazz-Hands

Theme: Shade (pronounced 'Shaday') has a chip on her shoulder because she is of mixed race. She allows it to become a problem, rather than an asset, until the day she meets Kathryn.

Setting: Saturday Dance Class

SEAL reference: Problem Solving; Good to be Me

Everyone agreed that Shade was the most beautiful girl in the dance class. She was tall and graceful. Her skin was the colour of a rich, ripe conker. Her tight curly hair was beautifully shaved very close to her head.

But Shade couldn't see any of it. She knew she was a good dancer, but she hated herself. Her mum was Ethiopian and her dad was German, and all that she could see was that she was mixed-race. She wore it like a badge and appeared very proud. This was ridiculous, and everyone said so, but no one could erase that feeling that she was in no-man's land. She felt neither white, nor black.

It wasn't that her mum and dad hadn't tried hard to teach her about both their cultures. In fact, that was exactly what they had done. Shade had even learnt some of the language of Welsh in her tiny primary school in Pantyffyncelin (*Pantafunkelin*). And in the school where she had now moved to in Cardiff, they had taught her about lots of different cultures. But she didn't feel at home with any of them. She could talk only of being 'mixed race'.

Then, last Saturday things got even worse. A new girl had turned up to

dance class; she too was very tall, but she was white. She had thick, straight almost corn-coloured hair. Her name was Kathryn. It was clear from the start that this would be a challenge for Shade, because Kathryn was a beautiful dancer too.

Harvey, the Dance Teacher, saw an opportunity that could change things for the better. He would get both girls, not doing ballet like a pair of swans, but to do the dance of the street, doing 'hip-hop'. He would get them to dress up in grunge-style clothing. 'It will be a really great picture to see them dancing together,' he decided, 'and it might even lead to some straight-talking.'

Straightaway both girls found 'hip-hop' difficult, because they were so tall and lanky, and straightaway it was clear that the girls were not comfortable dancing together.

After one lesson, Shade shouted out to Kathryn.

'You're useless! You're so tight and snooty, just relax and let yourself unfreeze, Ice-Maiden!'

Kathryn twisted around and yelled back, 'Really? Well, do you know what your problem is,

Miss-I've-got-a-chip-on-my-shoulder, you need to stop being so proud!'

The whole dance studio stopped to see what would happen next.

Harvey kept quiet and prayed for a happy outcome. He believed in both girls.

'You know nothing,' shouted Shade, pointing her finger and jabbing it towards Kathryn. 'It's easy for you to find your place, walk in, all confident and think you own the world!'

'Ha! So you think! You're not the only ethnic minority around here, you know. Stop wearing it like a badge to protect yourself!' Kathryn shouted back.

'If you say that again you might regret it,' hissed Shade, through gritted teeth.

Kathryn breathed out. Slowly she walked towards Shade. Everyone, except Harvey, was expecting the worst.

Kathryn lifted her hand. Everyone sucked in their breath.

What was she going to do?

But then to everyone's surprise, Kathryn held out her hand in a gesture of friendship and took Shade's hand in hers.

Shade looked as stunned as all the others felt.

'Meet your new best mixed-race friend,' smiled Kathryn. 'My mother is Russian and my father is Australian, now there is a mix-up for you! Isn't it good to be different?'

Everyone laughed which relieved the tension.

Harvey spoke up. 'Well, my lovelies,' he began in a mock Welsh accent. 'Thanks for trying that. But I'm afraid to say you are both rubbish at street dancing, so how about we try some jazz hands and do a piece from Chicago?'

The lesson worked fantastically, and proved to all who took part that in celebrating our differences we find our similarities.

Follow-up questions

- Why was Harvey willing to take a risk with the street dancing?
- What was the most helpful thing that Shade learnt from meeting Kathryn?

King Nincompoop Goes Green

Theme: Going Green to save the Planet. King Nincompoop is really enthusiastic about 'going green', but sadly he has misunderstood the whole concept and is in danger of making himself look very foolish. Only one small boy is brave enough to help him.

Setting: The King's Palace in the imaginary land of Nincompoopia

SEAL reference: Problem Solving

The Palace Court of Nincompoopia was in turmoil. King Nincompoop had had *another* idea. In fact, he had just announced to all his officials that he was going to issue a special new edict based on that idea that very afternoon. He would make the proclamation at the stroke of three on the clock. All his subjects, and he meant *all* his subjects, from the oldest to the smallest, must attend.

'What is he thinking?' wailed the Chancellor. 'Has he forgotten that Queen Tarradiddle is coming to tea this afternoon? How very embarassing.'

'She's always early,' sympathized the Equerry. 'And he will still be making us listen to another of his long, long, l-o-n-g edicts and there will be no one around to welcome her.'

But the King had spoken and so they hurriedly sent out word round the Kingdom.

At almost three o'clock, everyone (and I really mean everyone!) squeezed into the Great Hall to see the King. What a crush it was, some people, who were right in the middle, fainted in the heat, but the hall was so full they were still standing up, held in place by the bodies squeezed tightly against them!

Suddenly trumpets rang out and then it became quiet. The King strode in dressed from top to toe in... green!

Green hat, green shirt, green dungarees, green socks, green shoes, green underpants! He even had his face painted with green face paints.

'This will be even more embarrassing than I thought,' bemoaned the Chancellor, and he covered his eyes with his hands.

All the King's subjects were aghast. There were a few whispers and sniggers, but no one felt brave enough to laugh out loud, not at the King, for fear of having their head chopped off! (Or even worse, having to taste his food for a week! Did I mention that King Nincompoop's favourite food was Brussells sprouts!)

'Yes, yes, my citizens. You may well gasp in surprise and delight,' smiled the

37

King. 'Nincompoopia is going GREEN!' He bowed graciously before his subjects, absolutely sure that they would support him in this plan. And of course they did, for fear of getting into trouble.

'Good, good!' shouted the King. 'Now please form an orderly line. Tallest at the front and shortest at the back so that you can sign the pledge for Going Green before you leave the hall. Go home and paint your car and your shed green, then paint your house, yourself and even your bed green! By the end of the day, everyone and everything in Nicompoopia will be *green*.'

Everyone stood there, in total silence, looking at the floor to make sure they didn't laugh at the silly King, who clearly didn't understand that the true meaning of being 'green' was to save the planet.

'Good, good, off you go now, safe in the knowledge that King Nincompoop

and all of Nincompoopia are doing their bit to be Green,' and with this he turned to his Heralds and called, 'Trumpeters! Fanfare please!'

'Excuse me,' came a small, but determined, voice from the front. The Trumpeters paused, uncertain whether to play. No one moved. Who was this who was interrupting the fanfare for the King?

Timothy was not a brave child, nor was he cheeky, but he knew he had to do this – not just for the good of the King and the Kingdom, but also for the good of the planet.

Nothing was said for a very long time and Timothy began to quake in his boots.

Eventually the King bellowed one word, 'Well?'

Timothy swallowed so hard that he sounded like a frog croaking. His mouth went dry and he began to tremble quite noticeably.

'Your Majesty,' he began.

'Yes?' drawled the King.

'Your Majesty,' Timothy started again. 'I think it's really important about Going Green, but I wondered if before we do so, you would come and see the rainbow that we have made in my school. We have put lots of things in place to save the planet. We chose the Rainbow as our theme, because it always seems to represent good things and it looks so very jolly. Only now, if we are all to go green, it won't be seem quite the same. Will you come and see it, Your Majesty, please?'

After a long time the King spoke again. 'What kind of *things* have you put in place?' he asked.

He didn't sound too angry and this made Timothy feel much braver. So he told the King and the people all about the organic food they ate at school, which they had grown in their own allotment. How they all went to school on an environmentally-friendly bus or walked with friends. All about their recycling bins for a wide variety of waste. How they had a second-hand-uniform-sale, because children grow too quickly and hardly ever wear out their uniforms. He also touched on turning out lights when you leave a room, planting trees on a strip of wasteland to encourage wildlife.

'There are lots of ways to go green and to help save the planet,' Timothy explained. And he went on and on and on, until the King held up his hand.

'Stop,' he said very quietly. He leaned down and whispered in Timothy's ear.

'Do you mean to say that simply *being* green is not enough to save the planet?'

'That's right, Your Majesty,' Timothy whispered back to the King.

'Oh dear, oh dear,' said the King.

'Why not tell the people that you have decided to omit Phase One of the Going Green Project,' said Timothy, keeping his voice down, but getting braver by the minute. 'Tell them that first you are going to visit the school and pick up tips to help everyone with Phase Two.'

Suddenly a fanfare blared out. The King jumped up and bowed graciously… to Queen Tarradiddle!

'Queen Tarradiddle, welcome! You find me discussing the Second Phase of Nincompoopia's march to a completely, greener, environmentally-sound future.' And turning to Tim, he gave him a huge wink and said, 'Thank you, Timothy, we shall both be delighted to come and peruse the valuable work you are doing at Nincompoop's First Green School. Will you take my arm, Queen Tarradiddle?'

The Chancellor looked at the Equerry. Things had turned out well *this time*, but they would never forget the day that King Nincompoop went green.

Follow-up questions

- Why didn't anyone, except Timothy, feel brave enough to challenge the King?
- What ways of 'going green' do we have here in school?

Spare a Thought for the Teachers

Theme: It is Miss Timms' first day with her first class. The day is almost over and she is congratulating herself on surviving when she meets Norman and a whole new world of challenges meets her.

Setting: School playground

SEAL reference: Problem Solving

Miss Timms was a very new teacher. She had left University only in July and here she was in front of her very own class. Part of her felt strong and ready for the challenges that lay ahead, but all the other parts felt weak and wobbly.

Hundreds of 'what ifs' had gone through her mind.

'What if someone cries and won't stop?'

'What if someone says no, when I ask them to listen?'

'What if I forget the dates in history and muddle them up, telling the class that The Battle of Hastings was 1666 and The Great Fire of London was 1066?'

Poor Miss Timms, she hadn't slept very well last night.

Then, hardly before she realised, it was afternoon playtime and none of those things had happened. 'That's it,' she thought, 'my first day over and nothing will ever be so scary, ever again.'

She smiled.

Too soon!

Norman was storming towards her. He was still a good ten metres away, when he started bawling her name. 'Miss Timms!' he yelled. 'They won't let me play!'

Miss Timms swivelled round to face the direction that the unholy noise was coming from.

'They won't listen to me!' Norman continued, as he hurtled towards her with all the power of a charging rhinoceros.

Miss Timms had to skip sideways to avoid a full frontal attack! Which meant Norman (who was planning just that because it was what he always did at home) landed, with a thud worthy of a large sack of potatoes, on the playground tarmac.

'Whoops-y-daisy,' said kind Miss Timms. 'Up you get.'

She tried to pick Norman up, but he was having none of it. He tensed and straightened himself, like a plank of wood, so that, whichever way Miss Timms tried to haul him up, the other end was still firmly on the ground!

'What's his name?' she asked a little girl close by.

'Norman,' she replied and, before Miss Timms could use it, she added, 'Stormin' Norman.'

'What?' asked Miss Timms, too exasperated to remember to say 'pardon'. Her tidy hair had escaped and she was chewing strands as she spoke.

'He always does this,' the little girl continued, helpfully. 'Mr Wainright usually gets two hefty Year 6 people to help carry him indoors.'

Miss Timms didn't know any Year 6 people, hefty or not.

Miss Timms tried the soft, gentle approach. 'Come on, little man – up you get, tell me all about it.'

Nothing! One wooden Norman still lay board-like on the floor.

Miss Timms tried giving him some thinking time.

'Well, Norman,' she added after a while, 'if you are not ready to talk to me about the problem, I will leave you there until you are ready to chat.'

She pretended to turn away, but she was still in his eye-line, and she knew that he was peeping.

Still nothing!

Miss Timms decided to shock him into action by calling in reinforcements.

'OK, Norman, I am going to ask Helen to go inside and ask the Headteacher to come and speak to you. Perhaps it will be easier for you to discuss your problem with someone who you know better than me.'

Yes, you have guessed – still absolutely nothing from Norman.

The one thing that kept her going was the fact that she knew he was taking cheeky peeks at her all the time. This meant he was not badly hurt or even that upset.

The schoolbell rang to mark the end of playtime and Miss Timms decided on a gamble. All the children were standing silent in the playground, waiting for her instruction to line up in preparation for going back to lessons. She gave them the signal to go indoors. Then Miss Timms stood silently behind Norman out of his line of vision. She waited.

Nothing happened.

She waited some more.

Miss Timms had no class this lesson, which meant there was no one waiting for her. The Sun was warm and the breeze was clear and clean. She was happy to be outside for the whole hour, if that's what it would take.

Ah! She saw his muscles begin to relax at last, he was curious that she had disappeared and wasn't trying to cajole him.

Miss Timms took two steps sideways and hid behind the big yellow bins, as Norman began to sit up. She could see him, but he couldn't see her.

Finally he stood up and looked all around the playground.

Norman was dumbfounded!

Miss Timms stepped out from behind the bins.

'Hello, Norman, feeling better?' She ploughed on before he had time to answer. 'Bell's gone. Back to class, please!' And she marched quickly and defiantly towards the school door.

Once she got there she stopped, opened the door, turned, and held it open for Norman. She hid a tiny smile, as she realised that he had followed her, just as she had planned. Though he did look rather displeased.

'They wouldn't let me play,' he said through gritted teeth, as he passed her. 'They wouldn't let me be in charge and make the rules,' he hissed. 'And now they have all gone in and left me on my own.'

'Norman!' Miss Timms called in a kind voice. 'If you sulk for that long every time you don't get your own way and don't tell folk what it is that you are angry about, none of us will waste our playtime waiting and waiting for you. Don't you see that?'

'But I wasn't ready to talk to them,' he answered.

'Then that is your problem, not theirs,' said Miss Timms, gently.

And, because she had not grumbled at him, Norman actually listened and understood.

Not a bad first day for Miss Timms.

She had conquered a Norman and it wasn't even 1066!

Follow-up questions

- Why do you think Norman chose to behave in the way he did?
- How did Miss Timms manage to solve the situation?

Football Crazy

Theme: John desperately wants to make the First Team in football at school, especially as both his brothers had done so. But, after many disappointments, he has to face the fact that this is probably never going to happen. John has to look for different 'goals' to achieve.

Setting: Home after another bad day at school

SEAL reference: Going for Goals

The end of the school term was fast approaching and John still hadn't been picked to play for the school football team. He went to training every week and tried as hard as he could to impress Mr Herbert, but his name was never written up on the First Team board.

After another unsuccessful practice, he headed home. Once there, he threw his bag into the hall, kicked off his shoes and went to sit with Dog. Mum was still at work and his older brothers, both of whom had played in the school A team, weren't home yet. What would he tell them *again*?

He knew they would be full of advice: train harder, get noticed, play fair, keep plugging away and worst of all – set yourself targets, John, visualize your position, think when it will be – make it happen – positive thinking. He could hear all the voices now, pounding around in his head.

Dog put his head on one side and whined at him. John whined back. Dog pricked his ears and looked forlornly at John. He understood how sad John felt. He didn't know why John was so sad, but he felt it and sympathized.

John buried his face in Dog's soft, shiny coat.

'What can I do, Dog?' he asked. 'I'm the only one in my family not to play for the A Team – it's a tradition!'

Dog raised his paw and patted John's arm.

'I wish my life was as simple as yours,' John whispered into Dog's fur. 'I don't even want to be in the wretched team, I just don't want to let the family down.'

Suddenly he sat up straight and hugged Dog's ears. 'You're right!' he shouted. 'Dog, you're so clever, why didn't I think of that?'

'I really *don't* want to be in the team, so why haven't I realized that before.' He jumped up and galloped around the room from armchair to sofa, to dining-chair to the TV, shouting, 'Yippee, hurrah, thanks, Dog!'

Dog stood still. He knew he wasn't meant to stand on the furniture. Mum would be furious if she knew. Dog looked bemused, then worried and, groaning like Scooby-doo, he covered his eyes with his paws. John saw him, and decided to calm down.

Mum was home first and John met her at the door with the words, 'I've made you a cup of tea!'

'Really?' said Mum, sceptically 'Why? Have you broken something?' she asked, scanning the kitchen and sitting room.

'No, of course not. Really, Mum, you are so suspicious!'

They both laughed. John with joy: Mum with dread. But Mum was wise enough to wait and let the real reason come out in due course, as it usually did.

John went upstairs and started plotting. He made a list, he loved making lists – it made him feel in charge of things. His dad made lists – well he had, before he went away to work. Now he was only home one week in seven. Lists made John feel nearer to his dad.

The first list was 'Why I like football!' and the second list was anything else he could think of that might give him similar experiences.

His first list turned out to have three major features: mud, mates and being outside in the fresh air.

His second list was a terrible shock! The only activity that offered all three things, during school and after school, was the Allotment Club!

The Allotment Club! John stared at his findings. Oh no! Not the 'weedy nerds', as the footballers called them. Mind you, Mr Herbert had an allotment and it was Mrs McSharry who ran it, with the help of Mr Hyde. They were both OK teachers. And Mr Fisher (the student in their class) who was really good fun,

went along to help as well. He had told the class that he didn't want to teach indoors when he was finally qualified, he would like to work in one of those new Outdoor Forest Schools. That sounded pretty cool.

John's eldest brother opened his bedroom door, 'OK, mate?' he asked.

'I think so,' replied John, 'and, before you ask, no I didn't make it onto the team *again*!'

'No worries, it took me a few weeks – you know what they say, never give up!' and he made a victory fist in the air.

Just as he was about to leave, John began talking quickly. 'Actually!' he called. 'I think I should give up. I mean I've been trying for two years now.'

'Oh! Err. Rightio. You happy with that, John?'

'Yep!' said John, trying to be matter-of-fact. 'Yep! I made lists and it was obvious what I should do.' Then he suddenly pushed Edward out of the door and shot downstairs in front of him, calling over his shoulder, 'Tell Mum I'm in the shed. Let me know when tea's ready – I've got to get my wellies and stuff for after school tomorrow!'

'What's that all about?' called Edward. No answer came. John was out of sight.

Just as they sat around the table for tea, the phone rang – it was Dad.
'My turn to go first!' shouted John. They took it in turns, because the first person always got the longest chat.

Mum, Edward and Matthew all sat around with their mouths open, as they listened to John babbling away to his dad. He was as happy as a sand boy, explaining all about leaving Football Club, joining the Allotment Club and, there was no doubt at all that Dad would be eating fresh eggs for breakfast and fresh vegetables for tea, next time he was home – all courtesy of John!

'Who's next?' John asked, as he turned to hand over the phone.

'What?' John asked, as he saw their faces. 'Dad thinks it's a great idea, he says new challenges are the best way to move forward.'

There was silence from the table and looks that said, 'Are you sure about this?'

John laughed. 'Dad says I'll be the next Alan Titchmarsh with my gift of the gab!'

Everyone laughed and Edward took the phone. Mum gave John a quick hug and middle brother, Matthew, said, 'Very perspicacious, my lad – look that one up!'

Follow-up questions

- Why did John want so much to be on the A Team?
- Do you think it is helpful to set yourself goals when you really want to do something?

Maisie and Sacha

Theme: Maisie and Sacha spend most of their time arguing, always looking for the bad things and never the good in each other. Mum decides that they need a challenge that will help them see each other in a different light and give them something else to focus on, rather than their selfish selves.

Setting: School holidays, helping mum at Playgroup

SEAL reference: Going for Goals (self review)

'For goodness sake!' shouted Mum. 'I really am at my wits' end with you two. Every holiday it's the same, you bicker and argue as if you hated the sight of each other!'

The two girls narrowed their eyes and glared at each other with terrible, sneering faces.

'You see!' said Mum, in her most exasperated voice. 'You even look at each other as though you were a pair of… of evil-looking aliens.'

Sacha and Maisie both began at once, shouting over the top of each other, trying to convince their mother that neither of them was in the wrong.

'She's got my new hair bobbles and I haven't even worn them.'

'She took my lip-gloss and now it's got grit in it, from the bottom of her bag…'

'Enough,' said Mum, really quietly and in a menacing voice, that stopped the girls in their tracks and made them look at her instead of each other.

'Ooohh!' added Mum, as an afterthought. She let out a small gasp of air and her face looked as if a bright light had turned on inside her head.

'What?' asked both girls together.

'A brilliant idea has just shot through my brain and it solves all my problems in one fell swoop!'

She laughed and, as she walked away, she called over her shoulder, 'Be ready in ten minutes. You need scruffy, but clean clothes on, your hair tied back in your *own* bobbles and sensible shoes. Meet me by the front door, please.'

'But why…?' called Maisie, looking worried.

'What for, Mum, if we're only going to Grandma's?' Sacha's voice rose to a complaining wail, as Mum did not answer and disappeared from sight.

With one voice and in perfect sync, both girls said, 'I hate it when she does that!'

The girls knew that voice. The voice not to be disobeyed.

So sure enough, they were standing at the door ready to go, when their mother appeared from the kitchen.

She had three packed lunches and three bottles of water in her arms, she gave one set each to the girls and put one in her own bag.

'Mum, we don't need a packed lunch for Grandma's house, she always prepares something for us,' said Maisie.

'And if not, she lets us go to the shops and choose exactly what we want,' moaned Sacha. 'I might not like what you've put in my box, you didn't even ask me what I wanted,' she grumbled.

Mum said nothing. They all climbed into the car and sat in miserable silence.

'Good!' said Mum, smiling at them through the rear-view mirror. 'Dumbfounded silence, I like that, so much better than those utterly disagreeable little aliens. Grandma's not feeling too well today, her arthritis is playing up, so you can't go to her house.'

The girls looked at each other and both of them raised their eyebrows, as if asking each other where on Earth their Mum might be taking them, before *she* set off to work.

As if she understood what they were thinking, Mum said straightaway, 'You two are coming with me to Playgroup…' She paused. '… where you will see children of two and a half years old not sharing, not taking turns and not asking first. You can help me teach them how to 'play nicely' as we say… and maybe some of it will rub off on the pair of you!'

The girls were not happy. They had planned to have a great day at Grandma's, doing silly things like texting friends, painting their nails or straightening their wayward, curly hair with their birthday gift straighteners.

They had *not* planned to spend the day in some draughty old hall, running around after screaming, crying toddlers who had no idea how to behave themselves.

They both sulked!

'Oh! Very grown-up,' said Mum.

Six hours later, exhausted and ravenous, despite the huge packed lunches Mum had made, the last child had been collected, all the toys had been carefully organised into a very small space, the floor had been brushed, the kitchen was cleaned and made sparkling, and everyone was laughing and joking about the antics of the little ones.

The other staff talked about the wonderful steps forward that such and such had made in remembering his manners, and how kind so and so had been to the new little boy who, suddenly, at ten past ten had realised that his mummy was no longer in the room.

Next moment, as the workers all bustled through the door to get home to their families, someone was overheard to say, 'Gosh, those girls of Mary's are good, aren't they? They could come every day, so willing to work and so caring towards the little-uns.'

'And so patient and understanding,' said another voice, 'explaining everything so carefully to the toddlers. I bet Mary doesn't know she is born with those two lovely girls in the house.'

Mary smiled with pride and glanced across at her daughters to see if they had heard. She could tell by the smiles on their faces that they had. She also knew, that they, too, had learned a lot today.

She wasn't going to say anything and risk spoiling the moment, but all three of them knew that the girls finally understood…

… that you may disagree, but you don't have to be disgreeable when you want to explain your point of view to someone else. (Even if it is your sister you disagree with!)

Follow-up questions

- Why do you think Sacha and Maisie spent so much time arguing?

- Was their mum right to decide to take them to Playgroup? Why?

Mario is on Report

Theme: Mario is on report for bad behaviour and someone in class decides to make him angry and try to get him into even more trouble.

Setting: School

SEAL reference: Going for Goals (self review)

Mario looked at Umah. He wanted to give him a good shake. Indeed, if he had dared, he would like to have kicked him. Hard! On the shins! But that was out of the question, unless he wanted to be in even more trouble.

Mario was on report. This meant that at the end of every lesson he had to ask his teacher to sign a sheet, with a comment on his behaviour and his achievement. It had been given to him by the Headteacher, Miss Brierley.

The report was for two weeks, this time… Mario had been here before and more than once. But he still hadn't learned his lesson!

This time, he was on report for abominable behaviour in the playground and, of course, the whole school knew about his predicament. It also followed that whenever he met Miss Brierley, in the corridor, she felt the need to ask him how things were going. To be fair, she never asked about the whole week, just the previous lesson or maybe a morning.

Mario had never felt so good as this morning when Miss Brierley had stopped him and said these magic words, 'But Mario, you can't be good every single moment of every day. No one is perfect. And let's be truthful,

Mario, you do have a lot to learn about being well-behaved.'

Mario had looked at her in a disbelieving way.

'No, Mario,' she had half-smiled, 'even grown-ups sometimes lose their temper, make mistakes, get grumpy, say things they shouldn't. It's just that we must all try not to do it very often. Otherwise, people get really fed up with us and stop wanting to be our friend.' She had waited, but Mario had not responded. Rather he had looked like a small thundercloud ready to roar and rage at anyone who came near.

He had given Miss Brierley a look that said, 'See, I knew you were cross with me!'

'No, I am not cross,' Miss Brierley had said, cleverly interpreting his gaze. She had to wait a while for him to cool down a bit more, but eventually he did.

Then she had smiled at him!

Mario was confused. 'What?' he had asked.

'Mario, if I said that we need to learn the skills for being good, better, kinder people, in the same way that we have to learn our tables or spellings, one at a time, would that make sense to you?'

Mario looked baffled.

She had tried again, 'Today, Mario, I will be taking first lesson and I want you to be as good as you can be simply for that time. You know, come in quietly, find your reading book, sit in your own seat and read while I take the register.'

Mario had looked disbelieving again.

'Is that all, Miss?'

'Yes, that's all. We've dealt with the playground fight and you've had your punishment. But you won't turn into a little angel overnight – sooo – I will settle for a boy who is at least trying to be better.' She had smiled at him again. This was quite unnerving for Mario – he was used to everyone scowling at him pretty much all the time. But it felt like a weight dropping off from his shoulders.

'Now then,' Miss Brierley had added, briskly. 'First lesson happens to be Art and we both know that you usually manage somehow or another to spoil someone else's artwork. Agreed?' Mario had the grace to look abashed.

'Good, so after the register, I want you to concentrate on Mario's picture and only on Mario's picture for as long as possible and when you get fed up or lost, come to me with your work. OK?'

Mario had almost smiled.

'Yes, Miss.'

'If anything annoys you, take a deep breath, count to ten and find me quickly. Do we have a deal?'

Mario had made a high five for her and, when he said, 'Yess!' again, he had meant it with all his heart.

But now there was Umah, being sly, making fun of his picture whilst Miss Brierley wasn't looking.

It was really, really hard to hang on to his temper. He could feel it bubbling up and making him into a volcano ready to errupt. Mario was breathing in loudly and blowing the air out like an angry bull.

Umah knew he was winning and teased him even more.

'Pink flowers! Oooh! How sissy!' whispered Umah.

Mario breathed again and started to count. One number for every breath in and out. In – one – out. In – two – out. In – three – out. In – four – out.

He was taking very deep, very slow, breaths and surprisingly he soon felt less like a volcano. In – five – out. In – six – out. In – seven – out. In – eight – out. 'Miss Brierley!' he called, loudly. Umah scuttled away: the picture of innocence.

Miss Brierley walked over.

'Are you alright, Mario?'

He smiled. 'In – nine – out. In – ten – out.'

Miss Brierley gave him one of her amazing smiles. Her back was to the rest of the class. It was only for him.

She looked at her watch and silently counted down. '5 – 4 – 3 – 2 – 1 –,' she mouthed, and the bell rang for morning break!

Everyone else filed out to play, leaving their work to return to later. Mario waited. He had done it. He had met the challenge and been good all lesson.

'Well done, Mario. Success! A perfect ten out of ten!' said Miss Brierley.

Mario carefully lifted his rather wet and soggy picture.

'It's for you,' he said, as it dripped all over the floor.

'Sorry?' asked Miss Brierley, confused.

'The picture, the pink flowers, they're for you. Being good is easy in small chunks isn't it, Miss. I think I could be good for a little bit longer, you know.'

Miss Brierley never told Mario that she had been absolutely sure he was going to explode when Umah was mean to him. Oh yes, she knew exactly what had been happening all the time. She simply wanted to trust Mario and help build his self-belief. Nor did she ever forget to remind him, when she met him in the corridor, how good he could be when he thought about the problem carefully.

Some days were better than others for Mario, but slowly the two weeks wore away, and suddenly it was all over. He looked at his chart and realized that he had been good all week – without even noticing – and it felt fantastic!

Follow-up questions

- Was it fair that Miss Brierley didn't do anything, when she knew Umah was being unkind to Mario?

- Can you name some of the skills needed for us to become good, better, kinder people?

The Green Man

Theme: Living the 'good life' in rural Wales was great fun for three children who believed that they are free to roam wherever they wish. The day they meet up with the new Park Ranger changes all that, but only for the better.

Setting: In the local copse making camp (bivouacs)

SEAL reference: Going for Goals

Victoria, Francis and Louise were brother and sisters. They lived in a tiny village in the centre of Wales and although they were very different ages, there was no one else of their age in their village – so like their favourite storybook characters, famous bands of children, they decided to be the 'Gang of Three'.

Dad didn't live with them any more, so Mum had quite a lot to do. Consequently, they all had to help out, but really they enjoyed their extra responsibilities.

Victoria, who was ten, was really 'little mother'. Whenever Mum was working late, she took on the role and marshalled the other two around to make sure all was done before Mum got home.

Francis was eight, and Louise was the youngest, at three years old. But they all got on well and sorted things out together. Once their jobs were done, the Gang of Three went out to play.

Their favourite place to go and play during the long hot, summer days was 'The Allt' – a small forested area at the bottom of the valley, with plenty of undergrowth and enough tall trees to make the day cool and exciting. There they would set up camp and build a bivouac. Francis knew all about bivouacs from the book his Granddad had given him for his birthday, *Surviving the Great Outdoors.*

There were lots of silly stories going round the village about strange people or Wild Men in the Allt – none of which the Gang of Three believed. But they did occasionally hear odd twigs crack or leaves crunch and they would stop very still, like wild animals, and listen. After a while, assuming it was just a bird or a squirrel, they would use signs to tell one another it was safe to move on.

One lovely summer's morning, before Mum was even awake, the Gang of Three collected basic rations in a rucksack; bottle of water, bread and butter, wedge of cheese, teabags, sugar and, if they were lucky, a couple of biscuits or one Cherry Bakewell each. They didn't take milk for their tea, as it usually turned to butter, due to all the jogging and jumping around it had in the rucksack before they reached their previous camp. This was always the spot they had used on their last adventure. Having checked that all evidence of their presence was gone and that the site had returned to nature, they would set off and walk for an hour or so, before choosing today's site.

They had a strict operation once they'd found it. Francis located a source of saplings or young willow growth and set about bending them over and threading them into a dome-shaped den. Victoria dug a fire-pit and circled it with stones to prevent the fire spreading where it shouldn't. Once she had dumped earth all the way round, she would go and search for large logs. Little Lou knew her job was to collect kindling: dry grass and leaves, small sticks and twigs and bring them back ready for Victoria to light the fire.

They were a pretty good team, and soon the Billy-can, full of tea, was boiling merrily and they were eating toasted cheese 'grumps'. Never, ever, did tea taste so sweet, or sandwiches so good as the tea and 'grumps' the ravenous gang ate on their days in the forest.

You can imagine their huge shock one morning, then, when they heard an enormous crashing and pounding behind them in the forest. This was no squirrel or a bird, and there was a loud voice shouting, 'Put out the fire! Put out the fire!'

Suddenly a man they didn't recognize, who was dressed in all the shades of green, burst into their camp – he was still shouting and waving his arms around.

The three children stood up to face the Wild Man. They looked brave, but inside they were shaking with fear. At first they were silent.

Then Victoria gently pushed Little Lou behind her, and as the eldest said, calmly, 'The fire is completely safe – I have passed my fire-makers badge.' She sounded quite sure of herself.

The stranger stopped and folded his arms – he looked around surprised by what he had found. He was amazed at the completely professional way that this little group had arranged their camp. So now *he* was silent and stuck for words.

Then Francis stepped forward as well. 'We live in the village close by,' he said, 'and have been making camp in this forest for ages. But who are you?'

The Green Man looked flummoxed. 'Er who? Er Oh! My name is Dan, Daniel Davies, Forest Ranger, appointed last week,' he added.

But then he got cross all over again. 'You *should not* ever light fires in the forest,' he stormed. 'Don't you know how dangerous it is, you are being very stupid!'

He glared at the Gang. And that was the moment Little Lou decided to have her say. She stepped from behind the protection of the other two.

'Badge?' she asked, in her very best mannerly voice.

The Green Man stared at her. But Little Lou did not back down.

'Badge?' stated Little Lou, again.

Victoria and Fancis didn't bat an eyelid at this. Truth to tell they were used to Little Lou taking over occasionally. 'She wants you to show us your badge,' they told him.

The Green Man seemed less like a Wild Man now. He fumbled in his pocket, saying, 'Sorry, sorry, I didn't mean to frighten, you guys, um! Oh! Ah! Here it is!'

Just then, Mum appeared through the trees. 'Hi, Gang!' she called, happily.

'I saw your smoke and tracked your path. I've brought you some… Who's this?' she finished, pointing at the Green Man. Everyone spoke at once and Mum had to stop them to get a clear explanation.

'Oh,' she said, when everyone had had their say. 'I see.'

Dan the Forest Ranger looked at the family and smiled. 'I think the best thing we can do is to sit round this lovely fire and you eat your feast, as we get to know one another, don't you?' He looked at Mum and she nodded. 'I think we need some new rules about fires in the forest,' he added.

'We would offer you a cup of tea, but we don't have any milk,' said Francis.

'That's okay,' he said. 'I drink mine black, too.'

'They are pretty special and resourceful children,' Dan admitted to Mum.

'You don't have to tell me that,' said Mum.

'I can see,' replied Dan. 'Would it be possible for them to help me show other youngsters how to enjoy the countryside in safety?'

The Gang of Three smiled at Mum, nodding their heads. Mum grinned and agreed. 'I can just see them as mini-Forest-Rangers,' she said.

Follow-up questions

- What were the best things about being the Gang of Three?
- What might be even better when Dan joined them and made the Gang of Four?

Red the Black Labrador

Theme: Sometimes it is really difficult to understand why someone is not their usual happy self and we need to persevere to help them.

Setting: At home with pet Labrador

SEAL reference: Relationships (making people feel cared for regardless of who they are)

Red the black Labrador looked sad. He hung his head, his tail did not wag, he didn't rush to greet Hector, his owner, when he got back from school.

'What's the matter, Old Boy, have you done something wrong?'

Hector asked this question, because the last time he had seen the dog so crest-fallen was when he was a puppy. Then he was being trained NOT to eat the furniture, NOT to try out his new teeth on unsuspecting cushions and definitely NOT to pee or poo indoors .

Red snuggled up to Hector as if for reassurance. The dog seemed to be checking that Hector still loved him, but he couldn't say that, so Hector was only guessing.

'Everything's alright, Red,' he crooned, softly tickling Red's ears. 'You're one of our gang, we all love you to bits.' Red looked up soulfully, the whites of his eyes making him look even more sad.

'I know!' said Hector, jumping up. 'Walkies!' he shrieked like some demented pantomime dame. 'Walkies!' he rattled Red's chain. But Red just turned and crept away towards his basket, tail between his legs. He dropped down and curled up in a tight ball.

'It's not bedtime yet, Red', said Hector, amazed at this behaviour! He decided to resort to the ultimate fun thing. Food! He found the big spoon and quickly collected a can of meat, and banged the two together.

'Food, glorious food,' he sang, fully expecting Red to bound into the kitchen and dance around on his back legs, singing his own special barky version of the song.

Nothing happened. Hector banged and sang again. This time he warbled nearly all of the song.

(Sing here if you wish.)

Still, nothing happened. Hector crept towards the utility room door and carefully peeped around the corner.

Red lay there in his basket, still curled up in a tight round ball, his sorrowful eyes gazing beyond his master.

Hector crept along the hallway on all fours, speaking quietly and reassuringly to Red. 'It's OK, Mate. You can tell me who's upset you. I've checked the house, no disastrous accidents. Are you feeling poorly?' He stroked the top of Red's head. Red made a strange little groaning noise and snuggled up again.

Hector was flummoxed!

'If only you could tell me. I wish, I wish you could talk. Are you sad? Are you tired? Do you have a pain?' Hector's list went on and on, as if he hoped that, at any moment, Red would respond to one of his questions and let him know which was the correct guess.

Hector sat back and wondered what he could do.

'I know!' He suddenly thought. When Jimmy (his brother) was really small and didn't or couldn't explain himself, Mum asked all his friends if they knew anything.

'I'll ask Red's friends!' announced Hector.

Except of course, all his friends were either other dogs or his pack – the rest of the family – and only Rory, his older brother, had been in all day (revising for his exams).

Hector went upstairs and knocked on Rory's bedroom door. He didn't dare go in without permission. Rory was a really grumpy teenager. Mum said it was his hormones, his exams and his lack of sleep that made him so angry all the time. Hector thought that was just plain silly! He could go to bed at 7 o'clock like Hector and get all the sleep he needed.

Rory roared, 'Go away you little imp! I'm busy and, no, I will not reach the biscuit tin down for you!'

Hector gathered all his courage and opened the door unbidden. 'Out! Out! Out!' yelled Rory from where he was lying on his bed, not-looking one bit busy.

Hector stood his ground. 'No!' he said quite stoutly. 'It's Red, there's something really wrong with him. I think he's really poorly, he won't even get excited about extra food!'

Rory looked shame-faced. He thought twice about whether to confess or not to his much younger brother. Better to tell Hector than Mum, he decided.

'He'll be ok. It's my fault, really. I opened my door and he was asleep outside it and I fell over him and I think I stood on his paw. Anyway he cried out and ran off and wouldn't come near me, so I left him alone to sulk.'

'He wasn't sulking, he was afraid of you! He thought he had done something wrong!' announced Hector.

Rory looked in astonishment at his little brother. 'Oh,' he said, rather lamely.

'Oh? Is that all?' asked Hector. 'He was guarding you – you should know that, he always does it. He can't explain things, so it's up to you to let him know you weren't cross or angry with him and that you still love him!' Hector was amazed at himself.

'OK! OK! Later,' said Rory, his anger gathering, once more.

'No! Now, please!' added Hector. 'He looks so sad.'

Rory knew he was beaten. He tried to make himself feel better by sneering at Hector and, as he passed by him, saying 'stupid dog!' But Red was delighted to see him again all the same.

Later that evening, Hector talked it over with Mum. 'Sometimes,' she said, 'everyone finds it difficult to explain a problem and that's when we must make an extra big effort to understand.'

'Oh! I get it,' said Hector. 'Like the time when Simon wouldn't come here for a sleepover and I got sad because I thought he didn't like me, but his mum told you the truth that he sometimes wet the bed?'

'That's right,' said Mum, 'sometimes we all try to hide our problems. But it sounds like you really worked hard today, sorting out Red's problem for him, I'm very proud of you.'

Follow-up questions

- Do you think it is important to take extra thought to try work out why someone is feeling unhappy?
- Did Rory make the right decision to leave Red to 'sulk'?

What if?

Theme: Emma so desperately wants to be Narinder's friend that she tries far too hard to impress her and the resulting anguish convinces her that she has lost her for ever. Narinder's Grandpa is a wise man and soon makes everything good again. Emma learns that simply to be herself is enough.

Setting: Classroom and Narinder's home

SEAL reference: Relationships

Narinder was the most popular girl in the Class… in the whole school… and most probably in the whole world! She was tall and elegant, she was gracious and she was *always* polite. Miss Stafford, the Class Teacher, was always asking the children to be more like Narinder. You might expect that this would have made her unpopular, being teacher's pet, but she was such a really lovely person, that everyone liked Narinder. Emma wanted Narinder to be one of her closest friends. Sometimes she even imagined being Narinder's *best* friend. Life would be just perfect then.

Narinder was Emma's partner in Science and, in the group work, Emma always made sure that she let Narinder do all the interesting bits, while Emma just did the recording and the clearing away. Narinder always took time to say that she was the best Science-buddy anyone could want.

All this is to help you understand why on Earth Emma did what she did this fateful day and, why now, the only words zooming inside her brain were, 'what if?'.

Today she would have given anything to be back where they had been then,

and with Emma still being nothing more than Narinder's Science-buddy.

You see, out of the blue, it had happened. One day, completely without warning, Narinder had asked Emma if she would like to come over to her house on Saturday for the whole day.

Emma had been shocked, but of course she had agreed straightaway. Then Narinder had leaned close to her ear and mentioned, 'Bring anything you can to play with, all my toys are soooo boring!'

Immediately, a little panic started in Emma's brain. What could she take that would not leave Narinder thinking that she was the most boring friend ever?

And that's why Emma was now to be found, at 3.30 pm this fine Saturday afternoon, hiding herself away in Narinder's Grandpa's spice storeroom. It had seemed so easy to borrow all the things she thought might be exciting for her new friend to play with. She had decided that they could all be back home safely, before their rightful owners had discovered what she had taken.

Well, that had been the plan, but like all good plans that are not thought through properly, she had not factored in Narinder's brothers!

Consequently, here she was in the storeroom, running through a long list of 'what-ifs?' as she sniffled into her hankie.

What if she had not taken that wonderful box of make-up which Dad had given Mum for her birthday? But it was so amazing, it had every colour you could imagine.

Now everything was a dirty brown colour, like when your art goes wrong and you try to obliterate all you've done.

What if she hadn't crept into her brother's bedroom and taken his brand new Wii game console? But who couldn't help but be impressed with that! Hardly anyone else had one yet.

Now it resembled the box of wires and bulbs from the Science cupboard for use when they were making electrical circuits. (How did they get it in such a mess?)

What if she hadn't ridden her sister's bike over to Narinder's house? Her sister was very particular about her possessions, always keeping them immaculate.

Now it had a puncture in the front tyre, one of the brake leads was broken and the whole bike was covered in mud!

Emma sat amidst the strange new smells and unrecognizable rustlings of the storeroom. She cried aloud, safe in the knowledge that no one could hear her.

What on earth could she say to them all when she got back home? And if

she tried to explain *why* she had done it, she knew everyone would tease her and laugh at her. Even worse, she was also sure that Narinder would be horrified at her sneaky, underhand ways and wouldn't want to be her friend any more.

Emma was so busy working on the what-ifs, whats and whys that she didn't hear the storeroom door open. She shrieked and jumped, all at the same time, when she realized Narinder's Grandpa was standing in front of her.

'Hello,' said Narinder's Grandpa, 'I thought you were busy playing outside with Narinder and the boys.'

'I was,' stuttered Emma. 'But it all went wrong when… when… the boys…' she trailed off, unwilling to ease her own guilt by trying to get Narinder's brothers into trouble.

'I think I might be able to help you,' said Grandpa. 'You see I happen to know that my grandsons are really very naughty boys. They like nothing better than to tease Narinder and her friends, whenever they can. Now show me what has happened and we will see what we can do.'

Emma's heart soared. Then two hours later, when it was time for Emma to leave, Grandpa had sorted out almost everything.

The make-up case turned out to be an old one that Narinder's mum had given her to play with. The boys had substituted it for Emma's mum's new one.

The bicycle was one of their own which they had been using that day at the bike track. They had hidden Emma's sister's behind the garage. The Wii console did have a wire loose, but Grandpa said he knew someone who could fix it.

Emma felt as if the weight of the world had been lifted from her shoulders. Yes, she would still have some explaining to do and no doubt she would be punished in some form once she went back home – but she had also learned a valuable lesson: what-ifs cannot solve problems, mend hearts or even sort out trouble.

Emma knew that, in the future, she would think much more carefully, before she decided to do *anything*. She realized that what you choose to do must always mean that you have to face the consequences.

At the end of the day, Emma could only be grateful that Narinder's brothers really meant no harm when they loved to play practical jokes.

Narinder too was grateful that Emma was the best sport ever not to get upset by their antics…. Grandpa kept quiet. He simply winked at Emma and she knew her secret was safe.

Follow-up questions

- In what ways do we try to impress people?

- What was the most valuable lesson that Emma learnt during her stay at Narinder's house?

Abigail's Report

Theme: Identifying feelings, understanding what others expect of us. It is the end of term and reports to families are being prepared. Abigail is worried that she has not behaved as well as she could. She enlists Mr Steet's help to create a different report of her own.

Setting: School

SEAL reference: Relationships (identifying feelings)

Abigail's heart thudded, as she heard Miss Wigg's brittle voice crackling from the front of the classroom.

' … and, do not forget, Abigail, I am about to write the end of year reports and your parents will not want to read what I have to say – again!'

Why, oh why, did she have to be in Miss Wigg's class? There were two other classes in Year 4 and she had prayed that the children would be placed in alphabetical order. With a name, like Abigail Armitage, she should surely have been in Mr Todd's class. Loads of Sport, loads of DT, loads of Science and no 'namby-pamby' stuff like Drama and Dance. But she had had to go with Miss Wiggs *again*. Abigail Armitage, or Abi, as her friends called her, thought she had managed to survive the year quite well.

No letter had gone home when she had dessicated all the tadpoles in the classroom jam-jar, by forgetting to return them to the pond on Friday – leaving them in the full glare of the baking sun all weekend. This had resulted in all the water evaporating! When they were discovered on Monday morning, some soppy girls had cried at the sight of the little crispy black remains. This had infuriated Miss Wiggs even more!

She had even managed to avoid being sent home for the afternoon when she had waited around a corner to trip up her friend, Barry Dixon, but he had double-bluffed her and Abigail had tripped up Mrs Sponge, the Cookery Teacher, instead. Luckily she was quite round and seemed to roll away from Abi's foot – for quite a distance!

The Head was *not* impressed and shouted loud enough to win a gold medal! (Only a pretend fainting fit saved Abigail's bacon that time.)

Then there was the message on the answer phone which Mrs Briggs, the School Secretary, had been asked to leave on Abi's home phone, after Abi had knocked someone out in a game of Tag rugby.

'It's a non-contact sport!' Mr Trudge, the Deputy Head, had yelled, as he tried to revive the teacher, who had come with the opposing school.

The message said, 'Abigail has, today, exceeded even her ability to create confusion out of order. You will be pleased to know that Mr Trot, from Lower Houghingham School, has now made a full recovery and will be able to return to work next week!'

The message was sufficiently vague for Abigail to assure her father that the Secretary had meant to say 'order out of confusion', but had been a little confused herself.

But now Abi was doomed. Disaster had struck! Miss Wiggs was thundering from the front of the classroom…

'Today, Abigail Armitage, you have achieved that which no child from this school has ever achieved before… You have driven the Head to tape up his mouth, for fear of what he might say to you. You have sent the School Secretary home with a migraine, in fear of what she may do to you. You have lowered the tone of St Oswalds Lower School, within the Borough, for ever. How could you? HOW COULD YOU?'

Abigail waited. 'Please don't say it!' she was praying… 'Please… don't… say… it….'

But Miss Wiggs did.

'How could you 'accidentally' drain the Aquarium, and then hide the fish down the toilet next to the old staffroom, during an Ofsted Inspection – when you knew that they would be using that toilet?'

The whole class laughed; then stopped suddenly, when they saw Miss Wiggs' face.

Fainting wouldn't help now. Apologizing wouldn't help now, either. This was it: the grand finale of Abigail Armitage's time at St Oswalds.

'What? What do you think I can possibly write in your report, after the year we have had with you and your antics. I would like to see *you* try and find anything good to write on your report,' quivered Miss Wiggs.

'Now there's an idea,' Abi thought. Straightaway at the end of the lesson, she enlisted Mr Steet's help. He was the Teaching Assistant and he always seemed to understand Abi better than anyone else.

And so it was… that night… both Miss Wiggs *and* Mr Steet sat down to write their reports on Abigail's school year.

SCHOOL REPORT

ABIGAIL ARMITAGE: Age 8 years 11 months

SCIENCE

Miss Wiggs' Report

Abigail has not the first idea of the consequences of her own actions in practical Science. She must think ahead to avoid disaster.

Mr Steet's Report

Abigail has an interesting and innovative approach to practical Science experiments. She fully understands evaporation and desiccation. Well done, Abigail.

PE/GAMES

Miss Wiggs' Report

Abigail is a little too aggressive in Games and needs to control her natural instincts to win at all costs.

Mr Steet's Report

Abigail's enthusiasm for Games knows no bounds. She is willing to tackle the biggest obstacles with powerful results.

GENERAL COMMENTS

Miss Wiggs' Report

Abigail's bizarre sense of what is appropriate around school leaves a lot to be desired. She really must control her need to make people laugh.

Mr Steet's Report

Abigail's innate sense of fun has occasionally back-fired, but without her efforts the school would be a poorer place.

The next day, Abigail read both reports carefully with Mr Steet. She marvelled at how similar, yet different, they both were. She realized that her forgetfulness, her responsibility for others, her need to be on the winning side at all costs, could be good things – if only she learned to think first! It was like a bright light in her brain!

She could so easily be the Star in the class, instead of at the bottom. With a little effort, she could turn all this trouble around. One small change in Abigail, would easily result in a major change in everything.

'Wow! Thank you, Mr Steet,' said Abi. 'It's simple,isn't it, all I have to do is… STOP *and* THINK!'

Follow-up questions

- Was Abi right to be worried about her school report from Miss Wiggs?

- How could Abi have helped herself to behave better and to stop herself doing something thoughtless?

Grandma Pitchford's Birthday

Theme: Grandma Pitchford is about to celebrate a very big birthday and
Dan has no idea what he might give to her on such a special occasion.
He need not have worried as his choice turns out to be perfect.

Setting: Street party

SEAL reference: Relationships

Dan was four years old. He thought he was very grown-up. He was allowed to join in with his older brothers and sisters *and* with all their friends now, but on days like these, when they were all at school, he felt really lonely. There was only his mum for company, and she was always washing, ironing, cleaning or just very busy. And Dad wasn't much use either. When he arrived home from work early, all he wanted to do was read his newspaper. It seemed as if no one had time for him at all – well no one except Grandma Pitchford that is. She always had time for everyone.

Grandma Pitchford lived at the top of the street. There were only three streets in the whole village. The houses were small, red-brick and terraced. They had been built for the miners, who had worked down the local mine.

To Dan, Grandma Pitchford was the fount of all wisdom. She knew the answers to all of his questions and she was never too busy to stop and chat to him.

Now Dan knew Grandma Pitchford was about to be 90! Her neighbours were planning a street party and they intended to invite the whole village to come and celebrate on her special day. Dan was sure that everyone would want to come, because, one way or another, they had all needed her help through the year. Some came for her recipe for Winter soup, others for help remembering something from the past or about village history, still others to ask for a few flowers from her lovely garden. They had even asked her to look after the village once when practically everyone else went on a daytrip to the seaside.

Dan wanted to give her the perfect birthday present. But all the others seemed to have chosen the best ideas already. His sister Annie had chosen flowers. Jon and Robert had selected a picture frame. Mum was knitting a beautiful soft cardigan. The list went on and on. It seemed that anything he thought of someone else had already thought of it first!

While the house was quiet, Dan went up to the room he shared with his two brothers and he opened his special drawer. He reached his hand to the back and pulled out a small tin which contained his most treasured possessions. He opened it very carefully, in case everything should spring out and be lost under the bed or the chest of drawers.

He had: one piece of rather old string (useful if his laces broke); a half-empty crisp packet (in case he was sent to his room, hungry); and his best ever, most treasured possession, his beautiful brown shiny conker. This was ready for the day in September when he started 'big school'. He knew that it would impress the other boys!

But he still hadn't any ideas on what he could give to Grandma Pitchford for her birthday.

Very soon the day of the party arrived and Dan felt quite ill, because he was so sad. He still hadn't thought of anything.

He went up to his bedroom to hide away, but his brothers were sent to find him and everyone was cross because he was making them late.

Dan was given ten minutes to get washed, dressed and come downstairs or they would go without him.

Dan looked out of the window. The Street looked like a coronation for a Queen (or King). The whole place was decorated with flags and bunting. There were tables and chairs all the way down the centre of Co-op Street. They were covered in fluttering cloths, with jam-jars full of flowers spaced along the length of them, and there were piles of food heaped high on oval plates – all for Grandma Pitchford.

He could see the very lady in question, sitting at the top of the table, looking splendid in all her best clothes and her favourite hat to keep the sun off her head.

He knew he couldn't miss the party.

Everyone trooped along to the top of the table and gave Grandma Pitchford their gifts: flowers, cakes, a brooch, handkerchieves, lavender water, boiled sweets and even a pair of slippers. All very useful for a lady who was 90 years old today!

Eventually it was Dan's turn. He just knew that everyone would laugh at his present. The only thought that kept him going was that Grandma Pitchford would understand. He walked towards her with all eyes following him. As the youngest there, a few ladies felt it necessary to say, 'Ahh!' as he walked past. That made it even worse.

When he came to Grandma Pitchford's side, she gave him one of her fabulous smiles. Dan reached into his pocket and took out a small ball, that looked remarkably like an old screwed-up crisp packet. He gave it to Grandma Pitchford. He couldn't say anything, because his mouth was dry with fear.

Grandma Pitchford slowly unravelled the ball as if it were something very precious.

Her eyes lit up with joy when she realized what was in the bag! Everyone began calling and laughing. 'What is it?' 'Hold it up for us all to see!' and 'Oh! Dan!'

Very slowly, Grandma Pitchford stood up and held her hand straight for silence. From her other hand, she let fall a beautiful shiny brown conker on the end of a long piece of string. Then in her loving, gentle voice, she called out to all those present, 'I challenge anyone here to come and beat my conker – once we have eaten all this lovely food, of course.'

Once everyone had had their fill of food and pop, Grandma Pitchford set about cracking all the conkers in the village. At last she came to Simon Smith's. He squared up to Grandma with his already impressive conker – an 18er. He felt invincible against a little old lady!

But he didn't take account of Grandma's glasses, which magnified everything – so much so that she could see the tiniest little twitch of Simon's string and she was therefore ready the moment he pounced.

Immediately Grandma swung her conker and brought it down with amazing force. The birthday lady of 90 shattered Simon's super winning conker in one fell swoop!

Everyone cheered and laughed. They called out to Grandma Pitchford, saying she was the Conker Queen of Co-op Street! Even Simon Smith shook her hand!

The day after, when Daniel visited her again, Grandma Pitchford told him it was the best birthday present she had ever been given. Oh yes! She had liked all her gifts, but no one else had given her anything that was nearly so much fun or that had been so very precious to themselves. She knew it had been given with so much love.

Follow-up questions

- Why did Dan want to give Grandma Pitchford a really special present?
- Was his choice of present a good one? Why?

The Team Rolls Out Time

Theme: Inclusion, making sure that everyone is involved or looked after

Setting: Children being set a challenge, in a mock set-up, on another Planet. They have to work out how to get everyone home safely

SEAL reference: Relationships (caring for each other)

'What do you mean, there isn't enough time?' asked Cerith.

'Exactly that. We simply do not have enough time left, before we have to leave this planet,' answered Rhys. 'The choice is, we leave Angharad behind and the rest of us survive, or we stay to search for her and risk missing our 'window'. The last option will quite possibly result in all of us from this ship being freeze-dried, before two more pink moons have passed!' Rhys sounded exasperated and upset all at once.

Cerith looked stunned. 'You mean we have to choose between ourselves and Angharad?' she shouted.

'It's 'for the greater good', or some such twaddle. My elder brother used to say it all the time, that's when there were still people left who were older than ten in this Universe!' His shoulders slumped, as if he had the weight of every piece of space debris on them.

It was an impossible situation.

'But what if she is quite close by? Is there any chance that we could double the time we have left. We could then use half the time to search for her and half

preparing for take-off,' reasoned Cerith. 'Or even better, half of us could go in small search parties in all directions and the other half could stay on board to prepare the ship. That way we get twice as much time for *both* activities!' She beamed at her own cleverness.

Rhys stopped and thought about the new idea.

'You might have something there, Cerith. Call all the crew members to the bridge. Say it's an emergency!'

Cerith held her nose and spoke like a Dalek. 'All-crew-mem-bers-to-the-bridge,-as-soon-as-poss-i-ble. E-mer-gen-cy! E-mer-gen-cy!'

Even though her voice was all one tone, everyone recognized the command and gathered quickly on the bridge. A ripple of fear ran through the whole group, like the crackling of storm skies that they used to have on Planet Earth.

Rhys took control, immediately explaining the situation and the options open to them. 'Consequently, I want each of you to choose to be in one of the parties. Those who choose to go outside the craft and search for

Angharad, and the rest of you, who will begin to prepare the engines for take-off for exactly five minutes before the Blackness descends.'

The children parted, no one spoke, each had made their own decision.

'Good,' said Rhys, 'a fairly equal number for both tasks.' He looked at his wrist and the micro-computer. 'Thanks to Cerith's brilliant idea, we each have thirty-four minutes to do our job. But, please remember, we *will* take off five minutes before Blackness. Give yourselves time to return.'

Once again, no one spoke, no one changed sides. All that could be heard was the soft 'shush', as the doors opened and closed to allow half of them to leave the ship through the seal.

The searchers soon found themselves out in the burning, dry air of Planet Zylop. Only their Daysuits protected them and fed them with oxygen. BUT! Should they be caught outside after Blackness – when the temperature plummeted by 1000 degrees – they would instantly be freeze-dried. There were no suits strong enough for night patrols. Night patrols never happened.

Meanwhile, Angharad had been deep in conversation with a Zylopian.

'You mean you can control time?' she asked, amazed.

'Of course! Can't you Earthlings do this yet?'

'No! But if you tell me how you do it – we could save our ship!' she cried. She might have found the answer to all their problems!

The Zylopian helped her to transfer the Knowledge to her micro-computer, so she could then head back to her Spaceship with plenty of time.

But, as Angharad jogged her way back to the ship, she fell into a Thunder-pit. Tragically, she had been so pleased with her discovery that she hadn't concentrated on where she was going. It wasn't a deep Thunder-pit, but it had very slimy smooth sides, so it was impossible to climb out.

She was desolate and angry with herself for being so smug.

Suddenly she heard voices… Earth voices.

'In here!' she yelled. 'I'm in the Thunder-pit!'

Seven small faces peered over the rim.

Angharad made a decision. She tore the micro-computer off her wrist and flung it as high up as she could, for the others to catch.

'Take it to Rhys!' she shouted. 'It has all the information on it to enable us to roll out time.'

'But we can't leave you in there!' called Cerith, her voice echoing like thunder.

'You don't have time to worry about me,' she called back, 'return to the ship and take the Knowledge back to Earth.'

The others knew she was right. They left with heavy hearts. Cerith heard Rhys's words ringing in her ears; 'for the greater good!'

But when Cerith and Rhys talked together at the Spaceship, they knew the answer immediately. They would not simply take

Angharad's computer and leave quickly before the Blackness. No, they would use the Knowledge as soon as they could work it out. They would roll out time now and make this day last longer. Then they would have time to rescue Angharad and still be able to leave before the Zylopian Blackness.

Angharad couldn't believe it when, two Earth hours later, she heard and then saw a bunch of her friends, leaning over the edge of the Thunder-pit. They lowered a strong, rope ladder and helped her to climb up. 'I knew something good was going to happen,' she said.

They all laughed together, relieved that they had risen to the challenge of their leader. What a day! But what might their challenge be tomorrow?

Follow-up questions

- Why do you think Cerith wanted to rescue Angharad when they were all in so much danger?

- Do you think this type of role-play can help us to understand how to work together as a team?

Daisies are our Silver

Theme: Jenna doesn't like the changes that have taken place in her life – nevertheless she tries to keep her feelings a secret. But one day everything comes tumbling out and she discovers a new way of looking at things.

Setting: The new flat and the local shop

SEAL reference: Getting on and Falling out

Jenna lay awake in her tiny bed in their new flat. From above, she could hear people moving furniture noisily across the wooden floor. From below, she could still hear the row that had been going on ever since she had come to bed. 'Would it ever be quiet?' she wondered.

Jenna's mum and dad had recently separated, and now she had moved with her mum to live in this awful block of flats. She could hear Mum clearing away, before getting ready to go to bed herself. They both had early starts in the morning. Jenna had to catch two different buses to get back to her old school and her mum had taken on a second job, before her normal one started, to earn some extra money.

'It can't get any worse!' Jenna cried. She hid her head beneath her duvet and sobbed quietly. She didn't want her mum to hear. Her mum had enough to cope with.

Early next morning, Jenna and her mum both played 'Happy breakfast' and pretended to look forward to the day ahead.

At school, Jenna kept her secret too. She tried to work hard and to be good fun for her mates. She had told them that her Dad had got a new job and that, for the time being, till their new house was ready, she and her mum had gone to live across town. But it wouldn't be for long – so no, they didn't need to come and visit her.

Most people took her story at face-value, but not Mrs Jinad at the 'Sells Everything' shop, by the bus-stop near school. She knew all the children by sight and quite a lot of them by name. After all, she and her family had run this shop for years. That morning, Mrs Jinad noticed that Jenna didn't look her usual self.

Jenna had caught an earlier bus, so she now had some time to spare. She didn't have any money to buy anything, but at least it was warm in the shop.

'Hello, Sweetie, are you okay?' asked Mrs Jinad, in her lilting accent. 'I've not seen you in the shop much recently. I wondered if you'd moved away.'

Her kindness was all too much for Jenna. She had tried so hard to be the normal, happy-go-lucky Jenna, and suddenly it was all too much. She started to sob.

Mrs Jinad rushed around the counter to comfort her. She gave her a box of tissues and led her through to the back of the shop. She nodded to her husband to take over at the counter.

'You don't mind if Grandma Jinad stays, do you?' she asked Jenna. 'There are so many rules these days and we can't even be kind without risking trouble.'

'It's OK,' said Jenna, smiling at Grandma Jinad, through her tears.

'I'm sorry,' sniffed Jenna. 'I'm so sorry, this is really stupid ,isn't it?'

'Absolutely not!' announced Mrs Jinad. 'A trouble shared is a trouble halved.'

Jenna didn't mean to tell Mrs Jinad everything. But, strangely enough, in the nice warm kitchen, full of cooking smells and with the sound of soapy water going round and round in the washing machine, her whole story came flooding out.

Mrs Jinad offered the occasional 'Oh!' or 'I See', but she knew she only needed to listen quietly and let poor Jenna unburden herself of her cares and worries.

When it was all over, Jenna looked exhausted. Mrs Jinad knew sadly that there was nothing she could do to fix things for Jenna. Nevertheless, she began to tell Jenna her own story – about coming to a cold, wet England as a young bride only 17 years old. Of how she missed the warmth of the Sun, the colours of her own country and how for years she wished she was back in India. Until one day, when her dear husband had brought home a small pot of coloured plants. They were great big gerbera daisies. One was lime-green, one was bright pink, another deep yellow and the final one orange. She laughed gaily remembering the joy that this small gift had brought into her life.

'And do you know, from that moment, everything suddenly seemed possible. It was as if the Sun had come out. I could see all the possibilities of this new country, if only I would give it a chance.' She paused and looked Jenna.

'I'm not saying it has always been easy, Jenna, but you know once I started trying to see the goodness, I found lots of it – in small ways at first, then slowly it all came together – and look at me now.' She spread her hands out to encompass her neat little kitchen, their small corner shop, but mainly the happiness within it all.

For the first time in ages, Jenna actually smiled. She jumped up and thanked Mrs Jinad. 'You're right!' she laughed. 'It's true, I really can make a difference, if I just try.' She picked up her school bag, ready to go.

'Wait there,' said Mrs Jinad. She disappeared and came back in a moment with a box of gerbera plants, all potted up.

'On your way home, tonight, call in to collect these. They are direct descendants of the ones my husband gave me. Every year, I collect the seeds and propagate a new batch. I love passing on a little happiness.' Jenna did exactly that.

That evening she almost ran up the flight of stairs to the flat. There was so much she wanted to do.

Once inside, she flew around the rooms, looking for bright colours. She tidied, she dried the morning dishes and put them away. And as she did each job, she felt the grubby little flat come to life. She put on some gentle music to cover the noise from upstairs. She laid the table, took a ready meal from the freezer and placed it into the oven with some tasty garlic bread. Soon there would be a lovely smell, for when her mum came home. The warmth of the oven made the whole flat inviting and cosy. Just in time, Jenna heard Mum's key in the lock. She stood beside the table, with its bright yellow cloth and the pot of gerbera daisies. She was really pleased with what she had achieved.

The look on her mum's face said everything. They fell into each other's arms and laughed and laughed. 'Why?' asked her mum.

'Because I've learned today that it's good to be me, wherever I am,' said Jenna, and she pointed to the daisies.

Follow-up questions

- What does the phrase, 'a trouble shared is a trouble halved' mean?
- How can we 'look for goodness' as Mrs Jinad did?

I Want! Won't Get

Theme: A new boy doesn't understand the rules or the language so has double trouble fitting in with his new classmates.
Setting: School. Circle Time goes horribly wrong
SEAL reference: Getting on and Falling out (working together peacefully to sort things out)

It was Circle Time and Mrs Taylor asked the class to make a circle on the carpet.

Everyone knew where their place was.

Everyone knew that unless they had the Stripy Horse in their hands, they should not talk.

Everyone knew that they had to listen very carefully to whoever was speaking.

Mrs Taylor had often reminded the class that both these skills were equally important.

Today's problem, though, was that there was a new boy in class, called Alexi. He didn't seem to know any of this. Nor did Alexi seem to understand when Peter tried to explain that he could *not* sit next to Jonathan, because that was *his*, Peter's, place.

Peter usually liked Circle Time, exactly for this reason. He would dearly have liked to be Jonathan's best friend all the time, but that was Jamie – so Peter had to put up with sitting next to Jonathan occasionally… in Circle Time!

Peter tried really hard to make Alexi understand the rules of Circle Time, but Alexi just sat there like a stone statue, next to Jonathan, and did not move even one centimetre.

Eventually, Peter, who was usually very calm and sensible, got cross and simply pushed Alexi out of the way. Quick as a flash, he sat on the spot where Alexi's bottom had been only moments before.

Now Alexi was angry too, but he didn't have enough English words to explain to Peter why *he* wanted to sit next to Jonathan – so he too resorted to violence. Shouting as loudly as he could, 'No! No!', he pushed Peter and tried to squeeze between the two boys.

'This is my place. I always sit here,' argued Peter. 'You have to go and sit next to Molly!' he shouted.

'No! No!' screamed Alexi, even louder and pushing even harder. His hand was now under Peter's chin, which was hurting a lot.

Peter gave up trying to explain and with one almighty shove sent Alexi sprawling into the centre of the circle.

At that very moment, Mrs Taylor emerged from the store cupboard. The whole class was now in uproar, some on Alexi's side, some on Peter's. Others were just enjoying the show, laughing and pointing, but not helping at all.

73

Mrs Taylor clapped her hands loudly. (She never shouted, she said her voice was far too precious.) But everyone, including Peter and Alexi, knew they had to stop.

Except they didn't. No one heard or, if they had heard, they were naughty enough to think that they might get away unnoticed in the melee which was now Peter and Alexi having a full-on fight in the classroom!

Mrs Taylor was not pleased.

Suddenly she found and blew her PE whistle VERY LOUDLY! The whole class was startled into silence and stopped – immediately.

Very, very quietly, Mrs Taylor spoke to the class. 'Everyone please sit up straight. Peter and Alexi go back to your table and sit on your chairs.'

She waited. No one made a noise. Peter moved back to his chair.

Mrs Taylor had a look on her face that even Alexi understood meant that he should do exactly as he had been asked.

The silence in the room was deafening.

Mrs Taylor waited and then spoke quietly again. 'Molly,' she said, 'you have the Stripy Horse. Perhaps you would kindly explain to me what all that noise was about.'

Molly wasn't sure she wanted to, but she understood that Mrs Taylor would expect her to try her best.

'Peter was trying to explain the seating rule, but Alexi wouldn't budge. Perhaps he didn't know the words that Peter was using, I'm not sure. But he wouldn't even look at Peter and then Peter got cross and…' she fizzled out rather lamely. It was the best she could do. She hadn't even been looking at them, until she heard the shouting.

'Thank you, Molly. I think you have hit the nail on the head as people say.' She looked all round the circle, but she did not smile.

'Pass the Stripy Horse to Alexi, please, Molly.'

Alexi took the Stripy Horse and grinned at it. He laughed aloud and made clop, clopping noises like a horse's hooves on the road. He even neighed like a horse. Then he looked up expectantly. His eyebrows went up as if he was asking a question and he held the Stripy Horse out in the direction of Peter, and then he shrugged his shoulders.

'Marvellous!' cried Mrs Taylor. 'I know exactly what Alexi means – does anyone else?'

Four or five people put their hands up. They all attempted to put Alexi's mime into words.

'He likes the horse and he knows it's a horse, because he made the right noise.' said Dan.

'He wants you to tell him what to do with it,' added Annie

'He wants to know if he should hand it on to Peter,' tried Margaret.

'Yes, and yes, and yes,' agreed Mrs Taylor. 'How clever you all are and how clever Alexi is. He has only just come to live in this country, he speaks very little of our language but, when he is calm and thoughtful, he can let us know what he is thinking.' She gave Alexi a huge smile. He smiled back.

'You see,' said Mrs Taylor, and this time she looked straight towards Peter, 'we never need to resort to scrapping. We can all make others understand without fighting or shouting.'

Peter stood up and offered his hand for Alexi to shake. 'Truce?' he asked. Alexi understood the sign, if not the words, and smiled back as he shook Peter's hand.

'Please come and join the circle, boys.' She waved them forwards. 'Peter sit one side of Jonathan. Alexi, come here,' again she pointed, 'sit on the other side of Jonathan.'

Calm was restored.

'You see, there is always a peaceful way of sorting out our problems – a calm way of getting people to do what we would wish them to do.' She nodded at Alexi and pointed to the Stripy Horse and then to Peter. But she said nothing.

Alexi got up and handed the Stripy Horse to Peter. The whole class clapped. Alexi bowed a very posh low stage bow and sat back in his proper place.

Circle Time resumed: all was well in Class 1.

Follow-up questions

- Was it a good idea for Peter to get cross with Alexi? Why do you think it so quickly turned to fighting?

- How can we settle our differences if we have problems understanding one another?

Ratty and Rabbit (AKA Stop and Think)

Theme: One night Ratty gets himself into a terrible fix and no one wants to help. It is only Rabbit's kind nature that persuades others to forgive Ratty and be generous in the hope that he may learn the lesson too.

Setting: Life for the wild animals on the Farm

SEAL reference: Getting on and Falling out

Ratty and Rabbit weren't friends. It wasn't that they were deadly enemies, it was just that their paths never crossed.

Ratty was lazy. He liked to stay in bed until it was really late and everywhere was clear for him to go scavenging for odd bits of food. Whereas Rabbit was up, often before the lark, and as the dawn broke, you could see him settled, quietly nibbling away at the tender grass shoots.

Ratty was a thief. He would be out and about all hours of the night, scurrying here and there, stealing any food that was around. He didn't care whose it was. Whereas Rabbit ate an early supper of grass from the meadow then off he hopped to his cosy burrow for a long night's sleep.

Ratty was greedy. He ate anything that stayed still long enough: odd bits of vegetable, corn seeds, even bits of mouldy food from the compost heap! Rabbit, on the other hand was an extremely fussy eater, he only ate extra fresh green grass shoots.

Ratty was also cowardly. He would never search for food and eat it where he found it. He would never risk being caught by its owner. He much preferred to grab it and race back to his nearest hidey-hole. Why, if he heard as much as a whisker twitch he would be off! Whereas Rabbit didn't have a guilty conscience. He was as cool as a cucumber. He was also kind. He would stamp his large back feet to warn others, further away, of any danger before dashing off to find safety for himself. So, you might wonder how two such different animals came to be out together, really late one evening.

It was the end of a hot Summer's day. Rabbit was enjoying the last of the cooler evening light, when he heard the most awful screeching. Whatever animal was making it, sounded both afraid and angry all at once, decided Rabbit. His first instinct was to dash to the safety of his burrow, but something in the cry made him worried. He decided to investigate.

Of course, you have already guessed who it was making such a dreadful racket. Yes, it was Ratty! He was caught in a trap and he really wanted to escape and get back to one of his hidey-holes.

Rabbit felt rather scared of the frantic rat, so he sat quietly by the trap and waited for Ratty to notice him; though he had no idea at all how he might help the poor creature out of the trap.

Ratty shot from one end of the cage to the other, biting and scratching at the thin metal strips that made up his prison. He couldn't get a grip at all – his teeth were too long and they kept slipping over and around the wire.

Suddenly he stopped stock-still! He had noticed Rabbit. He watched and didn't move a muscle.

'Can I help in any way?' asked Rabbit.

Ratty was so stunned he couldn't answer.

'Can you hear me, Ratty? Is there anything I can do to help?' Rabbit asked a second time.

Ratty was now completely overcome – no one had ever been kind to him before.

'Th…Thank you,' he mumbled, 'but I don't think so. You see, it's a man-made trap and I don't think either of us will be able to work out how to get me free.'

'Wait a moment,' said Rabbit, 'I've got some clever friends who know humans quite well. I'll go and ask them to think of something for us.' And with that

he was gone, just a flash of his white powder-puff tail disappearing into the distance.

It was dark before Rabbit came back, and he was cold. He was also alone and looking very deflated.

'No luck?' asked Ratty.

'Well… I have to be honest,' began Rabbit. 'As I told them about the problem, everyone seemed keen to help, but when I told them it was you, Ratty, they quickly changed their minds.'

'Go on,' said Ratty, feeling slightly cross and hard-done-by.

'Well, first I asked Pigeon. She's quite clever, but you stole one of the eggs from her nest last week and she can't quite forgive you.'

'Hmmm,' said Ratty, slightly more angry and worried, 'who else?'

'Field Mouse, but you ate his stash of corn that he had hidden to keep him and his family fed through the cold Winter months.'

Ratty was not looking best pleased so Rabbit ploughed on quickly. 'Then I asked Worm, as I thought he could slither in and out and maybe unlock the cage, but you ate his brother last week and he's still too sad. After that I asked…'

'Stop! Stop!' shouted Ratty, getting even more angry and a lot more afraid. 'I see the picture. I've upset too many of the animals and the birds, so they won't help me. I understand.' Slowly Ratty began to realize that his thoughtless actions meant that, when he needed someone, he had no friends.

'Did you really need to do all those bad things?' asked Rabbit.

'No,' said Ratty miserably, 'I wasn't even hungry when I ate Walter the Worm, but you never know where your next meal is coming from, do you?'

'I do,' said Rabbit, 'mine just grows out of the ground, fresh every day.'

'But I can't live on grass, I need a mixed diet,' moaned Ratty.

'But you do like to eat seeds and old vegetables and they don't hurt other folk. As long as you collect your own!' added Rabbit. 'And I do think my friends might come and help if you made a promise to stop and think, *before* you eat everything you see!'

'You're right,' said Ratty, sadly, 'but it's too late. I shall probably have to stay in here until I die of starvation and I'll never have a chance to be a good rat.' Ratty began to cry real tears, but still he was full of self-pity. Which is why he didn't notice all the little creatures who had crept back to offer help – but only because Rabbit was a good friend of theirs.

Lucky old Ratty.

It took a little of Pigeon's brains, the Field Mouse's ingenious understanding of locks and Worm's ability to slither in and out of the trap, and they soon set Ratty free, safe and sound.

He could not say 'Thank you' enough times.

All the creatures agreed, however, that no thanks were necessary, as long as the next time he was hungry he would just stop and think! And they all chorused together to make sure he heard.

Ratty never forgot that night or those words of advice. He made sure that he told all his family lots of times too. He wanted to make sure they learned the lesson as well.

And that is why, to this very day, you will always see a rat hesitate before he eats anything.

Follow-up questions

- What lessons did Ratty learn from Rabbit?
- Why did the friends decide to help Ratty after all?
- How difficult is it to forgive someone who has hurt you?

'Samstan' – the Two-Headed Monster

Theme: Sam and Stan are twins and they are jealous of their little brother. They plan together to give him his 'come-uppance', but it all goes wrong and they are left feeling mean and horrid. They certainly learn a lesson about being kind to others if you want people to be kind to you.

Setting: In the car, both on the way to school and at home

SEAL reference: Getting on and Falling out

'S–L–O–W,' said Freddy very gradually – he was spelling out the word on the road ahead of them.

'What did you say?' asked Mum, squinting at him through the rear-view mirror. Freddy smiled back at her. She beamed at him.

'Did you hear that, you two? Freddy read the big word on the road – SLOW – he read it out loud. Clever boy!' she smiled again.

Sam and Stan looked at each other. Freddy was their little brother and the twins were fed up with him being adored, as if he were a genius!

Mum began to sing as she drove along. She was happy. She had thought Freddy was a genius before. He had said 'four' when she had been testing the twins on their tables. Mum had asked the question: 'What is two times two?' and Freddy had called out 'Four!'

Sam and Stan knew that he had only said that because it had been his fourth birthday last week and it was his favourite number. But Mum didn't see it

that way. She told the story to Dad that night, as though Freddy was destined to be the next maths whiz at school. No doubt she would also tell him tonight that Freddy could read. Now Freddy was probably destined to be the reader of the year too.

As soon as Mum had dropped Sam and Stan off at the school gates (watching them go safely inside before she drove off) the boys headed straight for their favourite bench and made plans.

As twins, they didn't really need lots of friends. They were like 'peas-in-pods' Auntie Flo often said. 'Two sides of one coin,' added Uncle Phil. The twins finished each other's sentences, thought the same thoughts, liked the same things. They were a powerful force together, and now they were out to stop Freddy before he got too big for his boots.

Freddy, meanwhile, sailed off with Mummy in the car. They were both smiling at each other. Freddy liked it when the twins had gone to school. He and Mummy did good things:

they went to the supermarket (where he usually got a treat); called in to see Nana Troy (where he usually got spoiled); went home for lunch, followed by an afternoon nap. After that they usually did an activity like cooking (where he was allowed to help – he especially liked licking the spoon). In fact, life was one big round of fun for Freddy.

But back at school, Sam and Stan had hatched a plan. They would teach him some really silly facts and even sillier answers. That should put a spanner in the works! 'What could go wrong?' they giggled, and they shook hands using their own special, secret handshake.

As expected, that evening, the whole family sat around the kitchen table eating tea. Mum told Dad all about their 'genius' son, Freddy.

Dad looked a bit sceptical. 'Are you sure, Maureen?' he asked.

Mum smiled at Dad, 'Oh yes! He's definitely our little genius alright. His new teacher will be overwhelmed when he begins school next week. Do you think we should go and warn her?' she mused.

Dad shook his head.

'How many people are there in our family, Freddy?' she asked.

'Four!' shouted Freddy. Dad looked at Mum as if to say – perhaps not quite a genius. It was obvious there were five people at the table!

'Oh that's because he sees Sam and Stan as just one person,' gushed Mum. 'That's how it makes four!'

Sam and Stan looked at each other – you could almost see the light-bulbs flashing in their brains, as they both thought of a new idea. Plan Number Two would be utilised before Plan One had even been tried!

A two-headed monster called 'Samstan!' Great!

Everyone at the table laughed, but each for a different reason.

Sam and Stan finished tea quickly and asked to be allowed to go to their room. Once there, they rolled around the floor, wriggling and giggling. Sometimes making monster noises, low and growly, other times reaching up looking bold and scary.

Stan took his belt off his jeans and tied his right ankle to Sam's leg. Sam tied his pyjama cord around their waists to help hold them together. They staggered round the room, bumping and thumping, roaring and bellowing. They were making so much noise that they didn't hear Freddy burst in. He wanted to find out what was happening. They charged around the room at top speed.

'Slow!' shouted Freddy, but the two-headed monster didn't hear him and then, to make matters worse, it fell on top of him. Together the monster weighed quite a lot and poor Freddy was badly squashed and all his breath was knocked out of him. He could hardly breathe.

'What's going on up there?' called Dad. The two-headed monster realized it had hurt poor Freddy. As they fought to extricate themselves and to quieten Freddy, Dad burst in.

'What have you done?' he cried. He shouted it really loudly. Dad never shouted, he was always calm and quietly-spoken.

Sam and Stan sulked by their bunks – eyes full of unshed tears, afraid of what they had done. 'Nothing,' sniffed Sam. 'We didn't see him', snuffled Stan.

'Be quiet!' shouted Dad again. He was afraid that the still and silent Freddy might be badly hurt.

There was a moment of complete silence…

'Two!' shot out of Freddy's mouth, like a cannon-ball filling the room. 'Sam 'n' Stan are two!' he continued, and then promptly burst into tears. Dad hugged him close and comforted him.

The twins realized at that moment that Freddy could actually count and that he might really be quite clever.

Dad saw their eyes and knew what they were thinking.

Very quietly, he said, 'No.' And the twins knew that he meant it. That voice was not to be ignored.

'Sorry, Dad. Sorry Freddy,' said the two-headed monster.

Dad spoke quietly to the boys.

'We will not know for a long time whether Freddy is a clever little lad or not, and it doesn't really matter one way or the other. He may become jealous that you, Sam, have made it into the football team or that you, Stan, can play your recorder well enough to be in the school orchestra. But if you teach him that you are jealous, what a miserable life you will all have, each trying to be better then the other instead of having your own goals and striving to be good at lots of different things.'

Sam and Stan hung their heads in shame.

'Sorry, Dad. Sorry, Freddy,' they said in unison.

'Sorry, Monster!' laughed Freddy, copying his brothers once again. He was blissfully unaware that they had wanted to be mean to him on purpose.

Follow-up questions

- Why do you think Sam and Stan were jealous of Freddy?
- Should Dad tell Mum about what Sam and Stan had done? How could both Mum and Dad help Sam, Stan and Freddy?

The Eagle and the Lion

Theme: The Eagle and the Lion both realize they have nothing to fear. They are giants in their domains. Unfortunately for them, the weather changes and after a great deluge, they are both in need of help. They find they have to swallow their pride and join together to survive.

Setting: Sub-tropical plain, South Africa

SEAL reference: Getting on and Falling out

Once upon a time, when only the animals, fish and birds roamed the Earth, there was an understanding between all species. They shared a common language they all could use, although they were all well aware who they could trust and who they could not.

All the creatures were peaceful and tried to help each other – all, that is, except the Eagle and the Lion.

Eagle knew he was the King of the Skies. He flew huge distances high, high up in the sky. With his amazing eyesight he could see even the tiniest creature, moving far away on the ground below. His nest was built on a rocky mountain crag safe from the rest of the world.

Eagle felt powerful, clever, in charge of all he could see. He was sure that no one could harm him or his family.

His piercing call travelled for miles and miles through the clear still air. He hunted alone, he had nothing to fear.

Many of the small animals were afraid of him though. Eagle had long, sharp talons with which he could grab them, and a pointed, curved beak which could tear them apart if he caught them. Whenever they heard his call or saw his shadow pass over, they would run for cover and hide.

And the Lion? Well, Lion knew he was King of the Plains. He wasn't afraid of Eagle or anyone else. He liked to rest in the shade of his favourite tree. All around the savannah, his amazing sense of smell allowed him to stalk his prey until he was close enough to pounce! His lair was no more than some tall grass or a shady tree branch. He was safe from the rest of the world.

Lion felt powerful, clever, in charge of all he could see and he was sure that no one could harm him or his family.

His deep, rumbling roar travelled for miles and miles around the savannah. He didn't need anyone. He had nothing to fear.

Many of the small animals were afraid of King Lion. He had long, sharp claws with which to grab them, and pointed, curved teeth with which to tear them apart if he caught them. Whenever they heard his roar or saw his shadow pass by them, they would run for cover and hide.

And so it was; until the year the rains started and did not stop. Day and night the deluge poured from the blue-black clouds that hung so low in the sky – so low that even the smallest animal or bird felt that they might simply reach up and touch them.

None of the creatures liked the rain. They ran for cover, but the rains carried on for days. Up in his mountain nest, King Eagle's feathers became so bedraggled, they hung limp and heavy. He was too water-logged to fly.

Down on the savannah, King Lion's fur stuck to his body and let the cold air in, making him shiver. He was too wet to run and his sense of smell was no use in the rain.

After three weeks of this, Eagle made a decision. He turned to his mate and said, 'I can stand this no longer. I am Eagle! Even if my wings are wet I am going to fly down off this mountain and hunt for food!' And before anyone could stop him, he flung himself over the edge of the crag, believing he was invincible.

At exactly the same moment, Lion stood up and shook the rain from his sodden mane. He said to his mate, 'I have had enough of this. I am Lion, I am going to search for food.' And before anyone could stop him, he charged out of the lair, also believing he was invincible.

Eagle landed on the wet ground with an enormous splosh – right in front of Lion, who skidded to a halt, covering himself in mud. The two kings looked at one another and then down at themselves. Suddenly they both forgot they were hungry and began to laugh. They giggled. They chuckled. They guffawed. They hooted with laughter at just how ridiculous they both looked.

'You know what?' said the Eagle. 'This is the best I have felt since this rain started.'

'Me too,' agreed Lion. 'But what on Earth shall we do now? We are both wet and starving. Neither of us can go hunting.'

They both thought hard.

'I know!' shouted Lion. 'If I help you dry your feathers, you could go hunting and if you then shared your food with my family we might all survive this dreadful rain!'

'How will you do that?' asked Eagle.

Lion thought again. (This was becoming a hard day.)

He looked cautiously at Eagle.

'Well,' he smiled, 'I could hug you close and keep you warm in my bristling, bushy mane.'

The Eagle took a huge leap of faith and crossed his toes (a well-known eagle safety precaution). He waddled slowly towards Lion, thinking this might just be the last thing he would ever do.

But Lion didn't eat him. He held out his paws and gathered in the eagle who burrowed deep into his furry mane.

'OK?' asked Lion. The only answer was a little moan of satisfaction as Eagle felt the warmth of his new friend begin to seep into his fragile frame. Soon Eagle was dry and he caught their first meal.

Years later, whenever they were hunting on the savannah, Eagle would swoop down and Lion would reach up for the strangest 'high-five' that anyone has ever seen. They never forgot the time when they had both had to work together to survive.

Follow-up questions

- Why did Eagle and Lion think they were invincible?

- Why did the two kings, Lion and Eagle, decide to trust and help each other?

The Little Frog and the Owl (AKA: Have you Met my Friend?)

Theme: In the excitement of discovering his amphibious nature, the tiny froglet forgets all the rules of the pond and, even worse, the rule about not waking the Owl. This leads him into a potentially dangerous situation and it is only his charm and 'joi-de vivre' that save the day.

Setting: The lily pond

SEAL reference: Getting on and Falling out

'Uugh! Help! Uugh… Drowning… Help…' was heard near the pond – followed by lots of bubbling noises and other swirling, gurgling sounds.

Suddenly with a mighty SNAP! a lily stem cracked and a tiny, hardly-yet-visible froglet pushed, with all his might, towards the top of the pond. He acted as if his life depended upon it. As he burst through the surface of the water, his cheeks were bulging and his eyes were tightly shut.

'Pahh!' he spat out the water and then sucked in a great big gulp of air.

Then he repeated this many times, his little chest heaving as terrible sobs wracked his miniature body. He was hardly as big as your little fingernail, but he was making a very big noise!

Eventually, he started to calm down and stayed still, lying beside a huge blade of grass. He was listening to the awesome drumbeat of his heart as it slowly came back to normal. That's when he heard a monstrous, fearsome voice beside him.

'Twooo!' said the voice, in a frightfully posh tone. 'What ooon Earth is all the noooise abooout?'

The newly-grown frog closed his eyes and kept *very* quiet. He wasn't sure, but he had a bad feeling inside that this might be The Owl, the one that everyone had warned him about… The Owl who was meant to be asleep during the day and out hunting for juicy little bites (just like a froglet) at night.

'I can see you, you noisy little green nitwit – lying there under that rather slim blade of grass. That's not good enough camouflage for *my* stupendous eyesight.'

The froglet shivered, 'Oh no,' he thought, 'my first day out, no longer a tadpole, and I have woken up The Owl!'

85

He said nothing, but a sorrowful tear trickled down his face, as he thought about all his family and friends that he might never see again.

'Harooomph!' coughed The Owl, as he cleared his throat and inadvertently let loose a pellet from last night's supper.

'No! No! Please don't eat me!' cried the froglet. 'I'm truly sorry that I woke you up. My mum will really miss me if you eat me, and there's not much meat on me anyway yet and… and…' By now he was really crying and shouting all at the same time, so it took him quite a while to realize that The Owl had flown down silently from his tree and was standing really close to him, making soothing twhoo twhoo noises.

The froglet tensed all his minute muscles, ready to leap off as far as his strong back legs would take him in case The Owl should take a lunge at him. His large black eyes focused on The Owl, waiting for the slightest twitch.

'Nooow then, nooow then,' said The Owl, 'as if I would want to eat a tiny little froglet like yourself! On the other hand though, I wooould still like to knooow what all that noooise was about. You did wake me up and I dooo find it sooo very difficult to drop off again during daylight hours.'

The little frog began to relax. 'Well,' he said and paused, 'if you are sure that you are not going to eat me?'

He looked at the pellet that The Owl had coughed up, and he was absolutely sure that the bones that he could see were wrapped up in some small rodent's furry coat.

The Owl saw which way he was looking and reassured him, once again, that all was well. He wasn't hungry at the moment.

'Well,' the froglet began once again, 'I was practising my new skill – breathing underwater and then out in the open air – but somehow it all went wrong, and my legs got caught in the lily-pad stems and I was trapped. Then I think I panicked.'

'Hooomm,' crooned The Owl. (Who was looking less like The Owl that the little frog's mum had warned him about and more like, well, more simply, just Owl.)

'Hooomm,' Owl agreed again, but this time he was also nodding his head in a very wise, owlish manner. 'Hooomm.'

'Hooomm, what?' asked the froglet. He was beginning to wonder if Owl was simply playing for time, deciding which way to pounce.

'It's like this,' said Owl, speaking in his master-like voice again. 'You have an exceptional gift there, young frog. To be able to live under water and to breathe in the open air is truly amazing. You and your kind are very special indeed.'

'Really?' asked the little frog.

'Oooh, yes! Do you knooow there are only a handful of creatures who can do that?'

'Nooo!' gasped the little frog, picking up Owl's intonation.

'Oooh yes!' enthused Owl. 'In fact the only, truly amphibious creatures are frogs, and erm, um, frogs and….'

'You already said that!' teased the little frog, becoming brave.

'I knooow, I knooow!' replied Owl. 'Just remember, it's the middle of the night for me.'

'I could help,' said the little frog, very quietly, for fear of upsetting Owl.

But when Owl didn't complain, he continued, 'When I was a tadpole, my grandad taught me that I had to stay indoors because a Great Crested Newt had nibbled the end off my tail and I thought I would never meta mor f…f… change into a frog!'

'Now I think I can help *you*, the word is metamorphosis.'

'Well, thank you,' said the froglet. 'Isn't it funny that here we are helping each other out and yet we are really opposites. You are a hunter and I could be your prey.'

'That's right,' agreed Owl. 'I am meant to be very wise and you are, are…'

'Not very bright?' asked the little frog.

'Oh nooo, oold chap, that is the last thing I was thinking.'

The froglet began to laugh.

'What is sooo funny?' asked Owl.

'You are. You called me 'old chap' and I've only just arrived today, as a frog!'

Suddenly they were both laughing, the huge old wise owl and the tiny new green frog.

'Is this what it is like to be friends?' asked the froglet.

'Yes. Yes it is!' smiled Owl.

'Now who would have thought it. We are so different and we live such opposite lives,' said the little frog, sounding very old too.

'That's true, but why shouldn't we be friends?' asked Owl.

'Friends,' repeated the little frog in a dreamy voice. 'Not just any friend, but my very first, brand-new, first-day friend.'

'We are very lucky to have found each other,' said Owl, 'and to have become such good friends. Now, when we meet again, I want you to tell me the names of all the other amphibians, please. I need a sleep now.'

'It's a deal!' called the little frog. He leapt back into the pond to find his mum. He wanted to tell her all about this unusual new best friend that he had just met.

Follow-up questions

- Was the little frog right to be afraid of Owl?
- How did two such different creatures learn to become friends?

Fire in the Forest

Theme: As the Sun rises, Vole smells fire, and warns the other animals to clear the forest. Fat Buck Rabbit, thinking it's just the sunrise, doesn't believe her and puts his family in danger. He finds it difficult to apologize, but Vole tells him that actions speak louder than words.

Setting: The forest

SEAL reference: Be the Best you Can be

As dawn broke over the forest, the brilliant orange Sun burst across the horizon like a ball of flame. The cool green dawn was lit up with hot glowing colours. Through the trees, Vole saw splinters of light race up the tree trunks. She watched them dance through the branches of the bare Winter trees, and thought she saw fire!

'Fire!' she screeched, at the top of her voice.

'Fire! Run for your lives!' Then she raced off, without another word, looking remarkably like a children's toy that had been wound up too tightly.

Immediately, all the animals and birds started to warn one another. They surged into action, a huge tidal rush of creatures trying to get out of the forest – every last one panicking, hurdling, hopping or flying in different directions. The noise was deafening.

'I don't smell fire!' said cool dude, Fat-Buck-Rabbit. 'Do you smell fire?' he lazily asked his family.

'We should ask Deer, she has an exquisite sense of smell,' said his wife, beginning to be worried. 'Don't you think we think we ought to be moving with the others now?'

'Ha-Ha! Deer has l--o--n--g gone,' drawled Fat-Buck-Rabbit. 'I'm sure it's only the sunrise, there's no need to panic.' He was comfortable and didn't want to leave his cosy burrow so early in the morning.

'But we'll be barbecued in our warren, if you don't get a move on!' whimpered his wife.

'We don't follow all the other jack-asses,' said Fat-Buck-Rabbit, convinced he was right. 'We're not sheep!'

Only a few minutes after the first cry of 'Fire!', the forest appeared to be completely empty. Then there was a rustle, as Hedgehog unrolled himself from his Winter sleep. He crawled out from under a pile of crisp dry leaves.

'Where is everyone, I wonder?' Hedgehog said to himself. 'Ah well,' he continued, 'Food first, friends second.'

But then the eerie stillness of the forest began to worry Hedgehog. 'Perhaps I've woken up too early,' he thought. 'Perhaps there's been a storm, it's always quiet after a storm. Perhaps I have woken up in a different world?'

Suddenly he realized that he was not alone.

Fat-Buck-Rabbit slouched out of his burrow with one very angry wife and the rest of the Rabbit family pushing behind him.

'Hey, Man! What's all the rush? Your whiskers on fire, Dude?' he asked Hedgehog.

'Excuse me,' said Hedgehog, 'But do you know where everyone is?'

'They've gone!' replied Mrs Rabbit. 'And so should you be!'

'Gone?' repeated Hedgehog.

'Yes, gone. They're all gone, every last one of them has gone! Except for us and my lazy, good-for-nothing husband.'

'Why?' asked Hedgehog.

Fat-Buck-Rabbit chimed in. 'Because of this fire we're having, man. Can't you see all of the forest is going up in flames.' He laughed again. 'Can't you feel the heat, man?'

Now Hedgehog was not Brain of Britain, but he was a sensible little chap.

'But there is no fire,' he answered.

'Yep,' said Fat-Buck-Rabbit, 'but nobody told that silly old Vole, when she saw the Sun rise this morning?'

'Didn't you think to tell everyone about Vole's mistake?' asked Hedgehog.

'He was too busy laughing at them all,' answered Mrs Rabbit.

Suddenly there was a whispering and a rustling, a whooshing and a crackling. The noise seemed to flow menacingly towards them.

'You laughed too soon, Fat-Buck-Rabbit,' said Hedgehog. 'Is this warm enough for you?'

And they all stood transfixed, as a mighty wall of flame gobbled its way through the forest towards them.

'Run!' squeaked Hedgehog – but the rabbits were already ahead of him.

At last they were all safe in the fields with the other creatures. 'You got here just in time,' they all commented, watching the smoke rising up from the forest. 'Why didn't you run with us?' they asked Fat-Buck-Rabbit.

'….because he is too big for his ears,' said his wife. 'He doesn't listen to little old Vole nor to his little old wife. He thinks he's *much* too clever.'

Fat-Buck-Rabbit looked ashamed. He needed to say sorry to his wife and to Vole – but he didn't know how. Fat-Buck-Rabbit hopped slowly over to Vole and clumsily patted him on the back.

'Oh, you don't need to say anything,' said Vole. 'Actions speak louder than words.'

Follow-up questions

- Why did 'actions speak louder than words' in this story?
- What was it that made it so difficult for Fat-Buck-Rabbit to say sorry?

Mrs Fuss the Dinner Lady

Theme: Mrs Fuss wakes to the magic of a deep fall of snow, but she forgets the joy and fun it brings and sails into overdrive to protect the children from 'danger'. In her efforts to keep them safe, she almost ruins the day.

Setting: First snowfall of the Winter

SEAL reference: Be the Best you Can be

Lots of the children thought that Mrs Fuss was just a bit too fussy. She fussed and bothered all day long. She double-checked and triple-checked, paused to think and then checked all over again.

One very good example of this was the day the snow came.

Mrs Fuss woke early that day and, even before she opened her eyes, she knew that something was different. The world in Sylvan Crescent was silent. She opened her eyes to find her bedroom drenched in a soft, strange light.

Now Mrs Fuss, as you have probably guessed, was not a young woman so she instantly realized exactly what had happened. But it hadn't happened for so long, that she had to leap out of bed and just check.

She could hardly believe her eyes. As she hauled back the curtains, a wonderful piece of Ice Art covered her windows. Beyond the frame, beautiful Acanthus leaves had been traced by Jack Frost. And beyond that, a deep covering of snow lay across the whole landscape.

Mrs Fuss's heart began to beat faster. In her mind, she was a child again. Age-old memories flooded back of snowmen, igloos, snowball fights, happy voices echoing along The Crescent. She could have cried with joy.

Needless to say, she didn't, because her next and most immediate thought was for the safety of the children. On Mondays and Thursdays, Mrs Fuss was lollipop lady at the village Primary School. (She was also their dinner lady for all the other days of the week.)

Mrs Fuss looked at her watch: 5.30 am Very early! But maybe Mr Dunn the site-officer would be up and about.

Mrs Fuss made herself a cup of tea and a very long list of jobs to do. She carefully dialled Mr Dunn's number.

'Ah, Mr Dunn, glad I caught you. I'm a little worried about the children today, so just to be helpful I've jotted down a few suggestions for you to put in place before they arrive at school this morning.'

Ten minutes later, Mr Dunn's head felt as if a swarm of bees were inside it!

Words tumbled around in a jumble of instructions: to salt the playground, make notices – banning the making of slides, the building of snowmen, any shaking of low branches to make mini-snowstorms, and definitely no throwing snowballs; heating set on high to facilitate the drying of gloves and hats… Or was that dogs and cats? Poor Mr Dunn set off for school in a terrible dither.

Mrs Fuss, on the other hand, felt a lot better, she had taken all the worry out of her day.

As she was finishing her toast, she realized there were lots of other people she should ring as well. She began with the Headteacher, reassuring him that both she and Mr Dunn would be on duty early, and warning him of all the dangers that she could foresee happening.

Twenty minutes later, the Headteacher fell back onto his snug pillow and pulled the duvet up around his chin! He had been well and truly organized by Mrs Fuss and wasn't sure he could face the day. 'Keep the children indoors all day?' the Headteacher groaned.

Mrs Higgins, the newly-appointed Head of the Highways Agency, was next on Mrs Fuss's list to ring. Mrs Higgins had been up all night marshalling her total workforce. But she couldn't promise that the gritter-lorries, and their now very tired drivers, would actually have made it to tiny side roads in the village, where Mrs Fuss's school was positioned, or that School Road would have been gritted.

'What!' screamed Mrs Fuss down the phone. 'Not sure if the roads have been treated. What will my little ones do?' she demanded. She imagined cars skidding, failing to stop, and children falling over as they crossed the road.

'I shall be taking this further!' she wheezed at Mrs Higgins.

After a quick rummage in the shed, she was dressed, ready, and off.

The snow crunched under her feet and, although her heart wanted to be glad, she knew she had a job to do and her head would only allow her to worry.

The Norwegian fur-lined boots, the three extra jumpers and the snow scraper she was carrying all conspired to make her very hot. The further she trudged the hotter she became.

Once she reached the school gates, Mrs Fuss stood there all alone. The whole world seemed silent. The snow was still gently falling on top of the already quite deep overnight snow. Mrs Fuss almost felt defeated before she had begun. But she took a deep breath and began clearing the snow!

It wasn't long before Mrs Fuss could hear the local children playing in their gardens prior to setting off for school. She saw soft snowballs cascading through the air, she heard the joy and laughter in their voices, she sensed the excitement of the first snowfall that some children had ever seen. She breathed in deeply and smelt the clean, clear, fresh smell of snow.

Tears trickled down her cheeks. Memories of her own childhood raced through her mind once more.

'What have I done?' she thought. 'What have I done?'

At that moment, she heard the Headteacher's voice, calling from across the playground. 'Well done, Mrs Fuss, now there is a good chance that all the children will be able to get to school and enjoy all the snow games that Mr Dunn and I have laid out on the big field. Those who want to can stay dry and warm inside to watch the DVD – jolly good idea of yours – and all the others who are dressed for the weather can play in the snow. What a marvel you are, Mrs Fuss, where would we be without you?'

Mrs Fuss pretended to brush away a snowflake that had landed on her cheek.

'That's right, Headteacher, just as I thought. Let the children enjoy themselves. Fun for everyone.'

The Headteacher gave her a great big wink and she knew he understood. She had simply tried her hardest to be the best she could be and that was enough.

Follow-up questions

- Do you think Mrs Fuss really did want to spoil the children's fun?
- Why did the Headteacher believe that Mrs Fuss had been doing her best?

Spot, Splodge and Smudge (AKA: Someone is Telling me Lies)

Theme: Three young Leopard cubs, who are virtually identical, try to trick their mum in the hope that they will never get into trouble. Mum cannot tell who was the naughty one. But it all comes unstuck one day, when Mum calls their bluff.

Setting: African plains

SEAL reference: Be the Best you Can be

'Someone is telling me lies,' said Mum, in a rather sad voice. 'How am I supposed to decide who did it?'

The three small leopards all looked at their paws and then down at the mess on the floor.

'It's no good checking your paws and claws,' said Mum, getting a little more exasperated. 'Why can't I rely on at least one of you to stand forward and tell me the truth?'

No answer from the three little cubs.

'Well, then, I shall simply punish all three of you and that way I will catch the culprit and the other two of you will just have to take it as 'one-you-owe-me!' Or is that 'one-I-owe-you?' Oh, well, I'm sure you can work it out. Perhaps over the year it will average itself out.'

'You can't do that!' shouted Spot.

'Oh!' said Mum. 'Is that because you didn't do it, Spot?'

'No! No! Yes! Oh! I don't know,' Spot stopped talking.

'What about you, Smudge?' she asked.

'I don't know who did it,' mumbled Smudge. She hid her eyes from Mum. Mum often told them she could see if they were telling lies, by looking in their eyes!

'Oh, well, that just leaves you, Splodge – what have you got to say for yourself?'

'Urm, er, dunno?' tried Splodge.

'Are you asking me to tell you that's an OK answer, Splodge?' coaxed Mum. She could sense a small gap in the armour of that tripartite animal called 'Spotsplodgesmudge!'

93

'You three always gang up on me,' said Mum, all forlorn. 'How am I ever going to teach the three of you right from wrong? How will any of us ever know for sure that we can trust one another to tell the truth?'

No one spoke up.

'Come on, Smudge, all girls together, you tell me.' Smudge looked horrified. The boys had only just agreed to let her be in on their games – surely it would be the end of that if she told. They had also taken the oath together, just like The Three Musketeers, 'All for one and one for all.'

'Can't!' she bleated.

Splodge and Spot glared at her. They even bared their tiny teeth and hissed a little, waving their skinny tails menacingly. Smudge flopped to the floor.

'Right,' said Mum, in the way, that implied she meant business. 'Enough is enough!'

She turned and raced off across the dry, arid grassland, and seemed to simply disappear into thin air.

The three cubs sat gazing intently at the point in the distance where she had seemingly vanished. After a while they began to prowl and pace around on their patch, feeling very uncomfortable.

'Where's she gone?' asked Smudge.

'Don't ask silly questions,' hissed Splodge. 'You saw exactly what we saw. How can any of us know where she's gone!'

Slowly they crept closer and closer together, snuggling up to try to keep each other warm. Their heads were bowed low, but their ears were twitching for the slightest sound.

The Sun set quickly and soon it was quite dark.

'I want my mummy,' cried Smudge.

'We all want her!' growled Spot. 'So stop moaning!' Smudge began to whimper.

'No noise,' cried Splodge. 'We don't want to be found by any predators without Mum to help us fight them off.'

'Oh! Don't!' whispered Spot, shivering. All three cubs cuddled even closer, their fine baby fur catching the cold, cruel night wind.

At that moment, they really did look like one animal, and a passing hyena (or whatever it was) decided it would make a very good supper. They heard cries in the distance, perhaps cries of 'Come and join the feast!'

'Oh, no!' whispered Spot. 'Now we *are* in trouble. I wish we'd told Mum the truth and that she hadn't left us alone!'

Of course, Mum hadn't left them alone. She had run far enough away to become indistinct from the grassland. Then she had circled round the cubs and slinking on her tummy had crawled back to within a few feet of the little terrors, and was simply waiting for them to know that they needed her.

Just as they did now.

'I'm going to tell Mum the truth when she gets back,' said Splodge. 'Then she won't get fed up and leave us alone in the dark.' The other two leopards agreed wholeheartedly to do the same.

Suddenly there was the most terrifying of growls, as Mum came flying out of the grasses that had camouflaged her. She tore around nipping the hyenas' back legs. She didn't stop terrorizing them until every last one had slunk away into the darkness.

She stood so tall and proud, glaring around her, still growling a low rumble to warn the hyenas not to come back.

Her heart was still beating fast in her chest and her ribcage was heaving in and out as she caught her breath.

'Wow, Mum, you are some scary cat when you want to be,' said Splodge, full of admiration.

'You do realize we could all have been supper for the hyenas, right now,' she told them.

They looked sheepish.

'You may well look like that,' she said. 'But if I wasn't around to teach you how to hunt, or tell you who are your enemies, you wouldn't last long, would you?'

They all agreed.

'You see how we have to trust one another, to listen and be honest. We have to be able to know who's telling the truth, or everything goes wrong.'

Suddenly, the cubs realized what Mum meant and that their silly promise, never to tell on one other, in the hope that none of them would ever get punished, was simply unworkable.

'If you have done something wrong,' Mum explained, 'whether by mistake or on purpose, you should own up straightaway and try to explain why. Then I can help you to grow up as good, trustworthy leopards. Do you understand?'

Spot, Splodge and Smudge, all said, 'Yes,' together.

They had learned a difficult lesson today. But they knew they would never lie to Mum again.

Follow-up questions

- Do you think it was fair of Mum to call the little leopards' bluff? Why?
- Why is it sometimes hard to own up when we have done something wrong?

Daphne and Ollie

Theme: Feeling too proud, feeling inadequate, making changes. The dinosaurs, Daphne and Ollie, need to sort out a big problem when Daphne gets over-excited. How can she improve herself?

Setting: School for dinosaurs

SEAL reference: Good to be Me

Daphne the Dinosaur had some amazing news! She wanted *everyone* to know how excited and proud she was. She ran into the Dinosaur School playground at top speed. She was looking for Ollie, her favourite teaching assistant. She desperately wanted to tell him her news. But, in her haste, she knocked over at least two tiny tots from the Nursery.

'Sorry! Sorry! Sorry!' She called over her shoulder, smiling at their mummies to make it alright. But, as she turned to smile, she accidentally swished her lumpy, spiky tail and threw at least three diddy Dinosaurs from Reception into the air!

'Hey, you!' they called. 'Come back, you hurt us!'

'I know! I know! I know!' she shrieked. 'But I've got news!' Then she giggled, as if that would make their bruises go away.

However, looking back at the Reception dinosaurs, she bumped straight into four Year 1 dinosaurs, who were practising their dance. The girl dinosaurs rolled around on the playground like fallen skittles, quickly becoming covered in puddle water and mud.

'Daphne!' they shouted. 'Just you wait!'

'Oops! Oops! Oops!' sang out Daphne. She had seen some of her friends on the big playground and desperately wanted to tell them her news. She waved her huge front paws with their long sharp claws, like a music conductor and, in doing so, managed to scrape the tops of six Year 2 heads.

'Ouch! Ouch! That really hurts,' called the young boy dinosaurs. They all began inspecting one anothers' heads for damage, while Daphne battled on towards her friends.

Sadly for Daphne, she was so excited that she forgot to stop before she reached them. She ended up as a huge green mountain, on top of at least seven dinosaurs in her class. In an effort to free them, she rolled backwards and forwards as she tried to stand up. The friends felt as though they were under a giant steamroller!

Even worse, they actually looked like flat pancakes, when Daphne the Dinosaur finally did manage to stand upright again.

Never one to be ashamed of her actions, Daphne burst out straightaway with her good news. 'You'll never guess,' she told them. 'No, of course, you won't, will you? No! Well, I'll tell you anyway.' Then she pirouetted around and around all the time, as she gabbled out her 'good news'. 'I am going to be a bridesmaid, for my mum's best friend, Beryl the Brontosaurus! How about that? I will be all in pink, and frilly and sequinny and – and – beauti-', she looked around '–ful!' she added sadly.

There was no one within fifty metres of her. All the little dinosaurs were pinned to the fence around the playground. Some were crying, others were huddled in fear. Some seemed to be lying on the floor, others, like birds of paradise, were hanging in tree branches. A few were like drowned rats, sad-as-sad could be and finally, it appeared that most of her classmates were now a pretty-coloured carpet, flat on the ground upon which she had just been dancing!

Slowly and ever so carefully, the grown-ups gathered up the battered dinosaurs. They brushed them down and hushed their tears.

It took a *lot* of shaking and plumping to reinflate her friends. 'It's like fluffing up your duvet, only it takes much longer,' said the School Secretary, looking around for the culprit.

Daphne, by now, was hiding in the Willow Weave. She was trying to make herself small enough not to be noticed. She sniffed a little and cried a lot, until she gave herself hiccoughs. But she still didn't come out.

Ollie had seen everything, as he had followed Daphne on her collision course through the playground.

He walked quietly into the Willow Weave. He didn't say anything at first. He simply waited for Daphne to stop sniffing and hiccoughing.

'What?' she asked, suddenly.

'You know exactly what,' said Ollie quietly. Daphne sulked.

'That won't work,' he said. 'You have done some really silly things in your time, Daphne, but this one is epic.' He was still speaking carefully and quietly.

Daphne looked like a deflated balloon and, for the first time ever, she began to look concerned.

'What am I to do?' she whined. 'How can I put it right?' she whinged. 'It's not my…'

'Stop right there, young lady!' Ollie whispered, ominously.

Everything went very, very quiet.

'You were excited?' asked Ollie

'Yes,' said Daphne.

'You were pleased?'

'Yes,' said Daphne.

'You wanted to tell everyone?'

'Yes,' said Daphne.

'What *should* you have done?'

Daphne thought, and thought, and thought.

'Oh! I know… asked Mrs Rigsby if I could tell my good news in Good News Assembly!'

'Yes!' said Ollie.

'But that would have meant waiting for ages,' moaned Daphne. 'It's not Good News Assembly till Thursday.'

'Yes?' asked Ollie, opening his large dinosaur eyes, exceptionally wide.

'Oh,' said Daphne

'Yes,' said Ollie, as if agreeing.

'That's today,' Daphne whispered.

'Yes,' said Ollie, most emphatically.

He looked down at one of his favourite young dinosaurs. 'When will you ever learn, Daphne?' he asked.

Follow-up questions

- Why do you think Daphne was too full of herself to care about her actions?

- How could Daphne have avoided all the trouble she caused?

Jeb the Giant

Theme: Jeb the Giant found a home on the landfill site and lived there for many years. The workers had been his friends but, once the site was full, they all left and he was alone and sad. Just when he feels most lonely, a strange little man appears, driving the largest truck ever! And a new friendship is born.

Setting: A landfill site

SEAL reference: Good to be Me

Jeb the Giant sat on top of the landfill site that overlooked the new National Forest. He was feeling pretty glum. He was up there all alone, because all the workers had gone. Their work was finished and that meant, officially, that no one would be allowed up on the site for five whole years, due to all the gases that were coming out of the pipes below.

All the waste that they had filled the hole with was now rotting so effectively that the Earth was 'burping'. And if this gas were not allowed to escape freely, then the Earth would have a pain – which could lead to an explosion!

Jed had almost smiled, when the workers had told him this, but even remembering their stories couldn't make him grin now. The workers had been his friends for twenty years or more. From that first day, when they had dropped that initial ton of rubbish on his head and he had stood up to complain, they had been with him right through until now.

He recalled what he had roared at them that very day: 'Fe-Fi-Fo-Fum! Who put this rubbish on my head?' He had had to push stray pomegranate skins and torn plastic bags from his thick, curly, red hair.

All the drivers of the dumper-trucks had come to a halt, every JCB scoop was paralysed. Even the wind stopped blowing and the seagulls stopped screaming. Everyone was terrified, thinking an explosion was about to happen. But Jeb soon managed to show them that he meant no harm, and they warmed to him quickly.

All the workers were sad when the site closure was announced. They would miss Jeb, but they knew they could no longer see him and had to move away.

Jeb closed his eyes in disappointment and started to doze.

A few minutes later, he woke up with a start. Jeb rotated his enormous head, slowly from side-to-side. He was looking for anything that was moving – nothing was. He cupped his great hand to his enormous ear, listening for anything making a sound – nothing was.

Then, out of the blue, a G.U.S, an unbelievably large German truck, with wheels the size of a small fairground ride, drove into view at the lip of the old quarry.

The G.U.S. enjoyed showing off. It was bigger than anything around and it had an air-horn that Midget, its driver, loved blasting. He did so right now, even though there as no one around here to get in his way. Or was there?

As if from nowhere, a huge oak tree came up, or rather down, in front of his windscreen.

'What the –?' Midget stood on his brakes and scratched his head. 'Where did that come from?' he shouted.

It was, in fact, the forearm of one very curious giant, though Midget didn't know this – yet! Just as he didn't know this site was now closed to rubbish tippers of all categories and that he shouldn't have been there.

'A hairy tree trunk,' marvelled Midget. 'That should have been recycled as furniture or at least wood chips – not thrown away in a landfill, a rubbish-that-cannot-biodegraded, site.'

As he leaned forward for a better view of this strange tree-trunk, something or *someone* peeled open the lid of his titanium, armour-plated truck, as if they were peeling the lid off a yogurt!

Midget nearly jumped out of his skin.

'What the –?' he shouted, for the second time, in as many minutes. He looked up and this time he really did jump out of his overalls in sheer horror. He stood shivering, beside his nothing-can-damage-me-truck, in only his boxer shorts covered with red love-hearts, a vest with 'Giant killer' written across the front and a pair of dirty black boots with steel toecaps.

His head was tipped as far back as it would go, without actually falling off his shoulders. Then he saw it. Way, way up high, in amongst the clouds, was a face so ugly, it would curdle your porridge.

'Hello!' he gasped.

'Yes! Hello!' Jeb called down to the miniature person, several feet below him.

'A new friend,' said the giant. 'Thank goodness!'

Jeb tried to pick up his new friend, between his finger and thumb. But Midge screamed and ran, hither and thither, trying to avoid capture.

Jeb pushed him down gently, with his first finger and, squirm as Midge might, he could not escape. He really believed this was the end of everything.

'Hello!' called Jeb again. 'Friend!' he added, firmly.

Midge couldn't believe his ears. How could he be a friend to this enormous person? He tried to explain to Jeb that they could not be friends, because of their great differences. It would be impossible to meet up or go to the cinema, or watch the football on the TV – because of their huge differences – 'Not least in height,' he finished, lamely.

'You don't understand,' said Jeb, and he went on to tell Midget why this was the only safe place for him to live as a giant. He couldn't go anywhere else. But, he went on, he still needed a friend, especially now that the workers had gone away and the site had been closed down.

'Closed down?' repeated Midget, and he asked Jeb to explain to him all over again everything about the closure of the site. Jeb even pulled out the plans the workers had given him, so that Midge could see what was going to happen to the site from now.

'I expect that means *you* can't come here again, either,' finished Jeb, all forlorn.

'Well, I'm sure I can think of something,' said Midget. He had already taken quite a shine to this amazing giant of the landfill site. And when he thought about it, he sometimes felt lonely too.

They paused and listened to the seagulls calling. Midge was a bird-watcher and heard other birds calling too.

'I know, why don't we meet up at the wildlife area,' said Midget. 'That's there at the edge of the site. You wouldn't need to leave here. You could simply lie down and no one would spot you. I could meet you at sunrise and we could listen to the dawn chorus together.'

So that's what they did. Come rain or shine, the Giant and Midget met up every morning. They talked and listened, and then listened and talked some more.

Despite all their differences, height being just one! They actually did become very good friends. Jeb felt that he was the luckiest Giant around, for he had a found a special friend in Midget! And Midget was sure he need never be afraid of anyone again. After all, he had a *giant* for a friend!

Follow-up questions

- What is the worst thing about feeling you are on your own?
- Jeb and Midget found a special place to meet. What special places do you like to visit with your friends?

What's in a Name?

Theme: Francis does not have time to have his hair cut before he returns to school.
His blond curly locks lead to lots of misunderstandings and confusion.
Francis decides to take drastic action to deal with the problem.

Setting: First day back at school after the long Summer holiday

SEAL reference: Good to be Me

Francis's hair was too long. He knew this and his mum knew this – but they had only just got back from holiday, late that night, and the new school term started tomorrow.

'No time,' said his mum, as if that would make it all right.

Francis knew better. The new term was not getting off to a good start.

He also knew that his name would cause trouble again. But his mum just said,

'Just say it's Francis with an 'i'!', as if that would make it all right.

Francis knew better.

He went to school the next day, begrudgingly. Why couldn't he have the day off and get a trendy new haircut to impress everyone?

'A day wasted is a day lost for ever!' said Mum, as if that would fix everything too.

Francis knew better.

At the school gates he hung back, looking for his friend Tim. He would protect him from the all the new kids in Junior school.

Suddenly Tim ran up beside him and gave him a friendly punch of hello – straight between the shoulder-blades.

It propelled Francis into the playground, he lost his footing and sprawled in front of all the new kids' mums.

There were shrieks of horror… hands rushing to pick him up… tons of 'There, theres!'… and then it happened! His worst nightmare came true.

One of the mums leaned forward and said, 'Oh! Poor little thing. She's bleeding from her hand. Ups-a-daisy, little love – don't cry! Be a brave girl.'

'I AM NOT A GIRL!' yelled Francis. 'I'm Francis with an 'i'.'

The kindly mum almost dropped him back onto the playground floor. Francis felt silly and angry all at once, and on the top of that he wasn't even sure that the woman had understood what he was trying to explain.

The day got worse. His new teacher mistook him for a girl as well and she really embarrassed him. It was PE first and she told him to change in the cloakroom with the girls!

'The boys stay in here where I can keep an eye on them,' she said.

Francis didn't even bother to be respectful (which was something his mum always insisted on).

'I'm Francis with an 'i' not with an 'e',' he blurted at her.

'Oh, Francis, I am sorry,' said the teacher. 'Please don't be angry – it's a lovely name and at least you know how to help everyone who makes a mistake.'

Francis knew she was trying to helpful, just like his mum, but it really was not helping at all. Had he not been surrounded by the class, he would have cried – not soppy tears, of course – but hot tears, of frustration.

But then he had a bright idea!

Next lesson, they all got their new exercise books – bright colours, clean pages, a new beginning – the teacher had said.

A new beginning! thought Francis, and in his bold, black handwriting, he wrote carefully on the front of everything she gave him:

FRANK THOMPSON

Frank Thompson – Literacy

Frank Thompson – Numeracy

Frank Thompson – Science, Spellings, Humanities, RE, Art, DT and on and on and on, and he felt *great*!

At playtime he told everyone that his name was Frank.

'Now that I am a Junior, my mum says I can use my 'grown-up' name.' Some were impressed. (Benjamin decided to be Ben. Jonathan decided to be the new, cool, Jon.) Others didn't care two hoots.

Tim said, 'Oh! OK then, Frank.' And they played happily together.

At hometime, his busy mum dragged him into the car, rushed him to the hairdresser's and pushed him through the door.

'Short back and sides,' she gasped at the man. 'Quick! He has to be at Cubs in half an hour, and he has to have his tea as well!'

Hair cut, tca catcn, Cubs attended and Frank finally had time to tell his mum about his day at school and about his idea to change his name, 'Oh! and please would it be all right for her to change all the names on his new uniform…'

There was a silence… followed by… not sensible phrases, not anger, not 'Don't be so daft!'

Francis was stunned.

There were *tears*, trembling on her cyclashes, big gulps in her throat, and then the droplets splashing down her cheeks!

'Oh, silly me!' she whispered, picking up a tissue.

Francis was dumbfounded. Scared. Upset. He had made his mum cry! But why?

After a few more gulps and some very noisy blowing into the tissue, she began.

'It's just that it was your Great Grandad's name – you never met him, Francis, but you are so like him with your blonde hair. He died in the war, a hero. He would have loved you so much, I'm sure.' She pulled out a photo showing the soldier's golden curls underneath his helmet.

'I didn't know how bad you felt about it,' she said, 'and I don't suppose the long hair helped today?'

Francis agreed and told his mum about the long and miserable day he'd had.

Mum gave him a great big hug.

'I'll have to chat to Dad. It's a long process to get someone's name changed.'

'NO!' shouted Francis, 'If it was good enough for Great Grandad, it's good enough for me! In fact being different is a really special gift, isn't it, Mum?'

'Yes, love!' she agreed, and hugged him so tightly, he thought he had stopped breathing.

'I must remember,' he thought, when he'd recovered. 'I must ask Gran to tell me all about Great Grandad Francis with an 'i' – Francis, the hero,' he thought.

Follow-up questions

- Do you think Francis was right to want to change his name to Frank?

- What is special about being named after someone else?

Chip Fat on your Ballet Shoes

Theme: Adapting to a new situation is really difficult for Georgina.
She has to learn quickly and take on board some enormous changes,
but feeling safe helps her to be brave.

Setting: Ballet School

SEAL reference: Good to be Me

Georgie's mother had always been a tomboy, so she couldn't really understand why Georgie wanted to dress up in pink frilly things and to go to Saturday morning ballet classes.

But once Georgie had made up her mind, her Mum didn't really stand a chance. Georgie simply became rude, cried, and shouted, until she got her own way. She knew that if she made enough of a nuisance of herself, Mum would always give in. It worked every time. Consequently, Georgie thought that was how she could treat everyone else in her world. But she was about to learn a very important lesson.

Never having been to ballet classes at all, Georgie's mum wasn't sure about the correct outfit for ballet, so she let Georgie choose. Consequently, when the little girl arrived, she ended up looking like a cross between the fairy on the Christmas tree and a jazz dancer. Too much tutu, too much sparkle, shocking pink leg-warmers, non-regulation tights and, worst of all, chip fat on her new, pink ballet shoes (Courtesy of a quick visit to grandad's Chip Shop, to show off the new outfit.)!

Mrs Abbott, the ballet teacher, had been running the Ballet School at Wittering Bagpole for what seemed like hundreds of years. She ran it as if it were the Royal School of Ballet in central London and was extremely strict about everything.

And yet, all the girls loved and admired Mrs Abbott and they did exactly as she asked time and time again.

Consequently, it was a terrible shock to both Mrs Abbott *and* Georgie, when they came face to face with each other that first, terrible Saturday morning.

Mrs Abbott was appalled by the fact that Georgina, as she would forever insist on calling her, was late. She was improperly dressed. The little girl called out the moment a thought came into her head *and* she had a stain on her ballet shoe.

Georgie was equally astonished that – unlike Grandad, Uncle Phillip, Auntie Pat, the Crossing Lady, everyone in the Chip Shop – Mrs Abbott didn't coo and smile as soon as she laid eyes on the-'vision-in-pink' that was Georgie.

'You are *late*, young lady. What do we say to everyone?'

'Dunno,' replied Georgie, in all innocence.

'Dunno!' Mrs Abbott's voice was immediately twenty decibels higher.

But, never one to be outdone in the shrieking stakes, Georgie hooted back, 'Don't you shout at me, only my mum can shout at me!'

For a second, Mrs Abbott was dumb-struck, and in that moment Georgie saw her chance. She leapt in, stamping her foot, pointing her finger and crying all at once. Every other little girl in the room was horrified at this display of such bad manners. It was something Mrs Abbott never allowed.

Mrs Abbott waited patiently for the tirade to be over. As soon as she felt a slight slowing down, she held out her hand like a policeman stopping cars, and, with her cane across her body like a Zulu warrior defending himself, she simply said, very, very quietly, 'stop'.

Georgie was so surprised that Mrs Abbott had not shouted back, like her mum did, that she fell silent. Every girl in the room held her breath and looked at Mrs Abbott expectantly, their tutus trembling around them.

Mrs Abbott realized that she had a lot of work to do with this new girl, but that did not deter her. Mrs Abbott enjoyed a challenge.

Meanwhile, Georgie was already planning what she would *not* be doing next Saturday morning – ballet class!

'Time for a break, gels,' said Mrs Abbott. She pointed elegantly towards the door. It was only ten minutes into the class, but not one of her 'gels' murmured. They simply filed out, heads down, eyes averted from the apparition that was still Georgie.

'Georgina,' said Mrs Abbott softly, 'what a pretty name. We have started off badly – got off on the wrong foot, as they say. We need to listen to one another, don't you think?'

Georgie opened her mouth to shriek again, but Mrs Abbott was quicker. 'Ah! Ah! My turn, I think?'

Georgie stopped and let out the big breath that she had just taken in. She sounded a bit like an untied balloon, flying around a room.

'Do you want to learn ballet, Georgina?' asked Mrs Abbott. Georgie looked confused: obviously she did.

'Good,' said Mrs Abbott, 'then I shall teach you. But to be a good ballerina, you have to follow *all* the rules, not just the ones you like.'

Georgie was sagging a bit, as she realized she was beginning to feel beaten. She didn't like doing as she was told, and she said as much to Mrs Abbott.

'Oh no!' said Mrs Abbott, rather taken aback at the mere thought of anyone being *told* what to do. 'I shan't *tell* you what to do, I shall *ask* you politely and you, of course, will then try your best to do it.'

'Oh!' whispered Georgie.

'Exactly,' said Mrs Abbott. 'I think we shall get on all right, you and I, Georgina. Especially if you promise never to wear your ballet shoes anywhere, except on my nice, clean, wooden floor. Will you come here in your outdoor shoes next week, please, Georgina?'

Georgie nodded silently. A little miracle in itself.

'Shall I speak to your mummy, after class, to explain our rules?'

'No, thank you,' said Georgie politely. 'I'll tell, I mean, explain to Mum. She's not very good at listening.'

'Hmm,' murmured Mrs Abbott. She wondered if that was true. But she said nothing, because she realized that Georgie was now ready to become one of Mrs Abbott's Saturday morning 'gels'.

Georgie, on the other hand, had no idea what had happened. All she knew was that she felt safe here with Mrs Abbott and that was a good feeling.

Follow-up questions

- Why is it often difficult to adapt to new situations?
- In what ways can we be polite to others? Why is it important?

If Only I Were Superman

Theme: Michael is feeling a bit low and is especially wishing he could do better, when he notices Great Grandma's slippers. Michael believes that they must be magic slippers, because Gran can do anything she wishes, especially after taking one of her 'power naps' whilst wearing the slippers.

Setting: Home

SEAL reference: Good to be Me

Michael had always admired Great Grandma's slippers, mainly because he thought they were the reason why, at 85 years old, she was still so clever and so busy! And secondly, because whenever she slipped them on and slept for a little while, she always woke up fizzing with energy!

That's why he decided that, the first time he had a chance, he would try them on for himself. Even though Michael was only six years old, he knew his feet were only one size smaller than Gran's. She was tiny all over. 'I'm nearly as big as her,' he thought, 'but she can do so much more to help than I can.'

On the 'Great Day' in question, Gran had disappeared, full of energy, following her usual snooze, and Michael sat in her chair and slipped his feet into the 'magic slippers' as he had come to call them.

He began to feel drowsy.

Oh no! The slippers were making him fall asleep and he certainly didn't want to do that! Gran only did that because she was old.

He jumped up and flung open a window to let in lots of fresh air, then he looked down at the slippers which were still on his feet and started waving his hands.

'Now show me your magic!' he commanded.

… and they did…

Michael had the strongest feeling that he was falling… falling through Space… through the floor, which was soft as marshmallow… through the ground, not hard but hollow with a warm wind blowing across his face… He had but one moment to realize that he was not afraid, before he felt as if he were being gently lowered onto a blanket as soft and soft as a cloud should be.

He began looking around – but there was nothing to see – just a blue light coming towards him, *very* quickly! He shut his eyes.

And with that he landed. After a while, he realized his eyes were still closed which explained why he hadn't seen anything yet. But now he was too scared to open them!

'Don't be silly!' he scolded himself. He counted to three and opened his eyes, before he could change his mind.

There he was, sitting all alone in Great Gran's chair.

Michael felt as if he had had the most amazing experience – the very best dream you could ever have had. He felt as brave as Batman and Superman rolled into one. He felt all-powerful, all-good, knowing everyone would admire and trust him. There were no problems that he felt he couldn't sort out.

Well, maybe his friends' or little sister's problems to begin with. Straightaway, he found Sophie's lost toy rabbit, while she was busy howling and Mum was busy worrying how they would get her to go to sleep that night without it.

Michael wondered how this had happened or if Great Grandma's slippers really were magical in some way? Whenever he put them on, it felt like he'd had this amazing dream.

One day, he was brave enough to tell Gran everything and asked her to explain.

'Oh, that's easy, Michael!' she grinned, mischievously. 'The slippers are so comfy that you can't help but take a power-nap. You see, your night sleep is long and deep. It allows your brain to rest and work its way through the day's problems. You will often sleep for a long time after your dream-sleep, which is why you can rarely recall anything. Whereas in the daytime, after a little power-nap, the thoughts or dreams are still fresh in your mind so you can recall them and sort things out.'

Michael didn't look as though this explanation was enough. Gran continued, 'Your brain is like an extremely complicated version of your Dad's best computer, only with much more power. Sleep allows the brain's version of Google to answer all your questions, problems, fears and hopes. Power naps do the same.'

So whenever Michael was feeling low, he took a power-nap in Great Gran's slippers. He didn't become Superman. But he really enjoyed being like her, full of vim and vigour, helping anyone who needed a hand.

The most important thing he had learned from all this, though, was that even if he couldn't always change the problem, with a good sleep or power nap, he could always be part of the solution!

Follow-up questions

- Why is sleep so very important?
- Do you think that Gran's slippers really were special?

Please Listen

Theme: When Tracey joins a class of really well-integrated children from so many different homes and places, they cannot understand why she gets so angry and demands her own way. But the truth is they are missing the obvious. Then, by letting her be independent, they find something really special.

Setting: School

SEAL reference: Good to be Me

In our class, there are lots of children from different places. There are lots of children who are different colours. There are lots of children from different faiths, and there are lots of children from different-sized family groups.

My best friend is Derek. He's Chinese and has four brothers all older than him. I asked him why all his brothers have Chinese names and he has an English name, but he said he doesn't know and that he's not bothered. He also believes that he was age one when he was born and tells everyone he is nine going on ten, not like the rest of us: eight going on nine! Derek doesn't argue, if you tell him that's daft, he just shrugs his shoulders and smiles at you. 'OK,' he says.

That's why I like Derek. He doesn't mind if you don't agree with him.

Derek and I have a whole gang of friends and we are all different in so many ways. Vinod is Indian. He's quiet but he knows really good jokes. Pieter is from Germany. He's in the country because his mum and dad are working here for five years. They've exchanged with someone, he's not sure who, and he's brilliant at maths.

Janet has Down's Syndrome and I've never met anyone who is so happy all day long. You can rely on Janet if you're a bit down and grumpy.

Jackson is the best sportsman in the school, even better than the Year 6 boys. He's our supreme athlete, but he was born in Bolton and he's got a really funny accent. (His mum and dad come from Ghana.) Mind you, he laughs at my accent too and we try to copy each other.

So, as you can see we are a real mixed bunch in Class 4. Mrs Smith, the cook, calls us her 'Fruit Salad'. She's great! She came in the other day to teach us how to cook a pizza from scratch.

Yesterday a new girl started in our class. Her name is Tracey. She lives near me, on my road, in fact. She's always been to a different school before, but now she has turned up here. I gave her a smile and a nod to let her know I recognized her, though nothing else, I mean, she's a *girl*! What would my mates think?

I didn't know, but Teacher explained that Tracey had been born deaf, so she couldn't hear or learn to speak, but that she uses sign-language. Tracey showed us how to say 'hello' in sign language. It was good fun and we all used the sign to say 'hello' back to her.

I noticed at playtime that Janet was looking after Tracey. She was showing her where everything was, introducing her to lots of people. Good old Janet, always helpful.

Now Derek and I stopped off each day to check that no one had 'moved in' on our special den area. It was often too wet and soggy to go in, but you have to keep tabs on your den, there are always others who might see its value and try to take over.

Today the wet Spring weather had gone and Summer was buzzing with insects and butterflies. The leaves had grown thick and dense and they had covered our den to make a cool shady green space in which to loll around in the long, lunchtime play.

You can imagine our surprise then, when we arrived to find Tracey in the den. At first I thought she was asleep, she was lying so still on the ground. But when she saw us she jumped up and started signing frantically at us. Now we hadn't had time to learn much from Mr Blick, the Makaton Teacher, who was coming in to help us 'talk' to Tracey, so we were lost. This was all new stuff.

She was really worked up and she tried to push Derek out of our den. As you know, Derek is a peaceable lad normally, but he took offence at this.

'No!' he shouted back, making a clear sign to ensure Tracey knew what he meant. I must tell you, I was very surprised, this was not like Derek at all. Vinod just stood quietly and watched.

Tracey frantically signed again still trying to push us out of *our* den. Derek and I shook our heads, but she was too ruffled to understand.

Derek and I looked at each other. No point in staying and trying anything else. We would have to go fetch the teacher-on-duty. Fortunately, it was Mr Blick.

When we got back, Tracey was guarding the entrance and she began signing really quickly as before.

'See, Mr Blick,' said Derek, 'she might as well be talking Chinese for all we can understand!' Suddenly we all laughed. Tracey looked dumbfounded.

'You *are* Chinese, Derek,' said Mr Blick.

'I know, but I can't speak it, I was born *here*, you know!'

Mr Blick laughed again and then looked intently at Tracey. He nodded his head as Tracey made the same signs again. 'Ah! Yes, indeed.' He turned to us. 'Tracey is signing, 'Please listen!' She has found something really special and we must be very quiet,' he said.

We all looked at Tracey and she signed for silence putting her finger over her lips.

'OK,' whispered Mr Blick. 'We need to be quiet and follow Tracey,' and so we progressed a little further.

Carefully we all crept into the den, even all six feet of Mr Blick.

She pointed to the back corner and there we saw a small broken flower pot and inside a nest of straw holding three baby birds.

Tracey calmly signed the letters R.E.D – red – and rubbed her chest.

'Oh… Robin Red Breast,' whispered Mr Blick. 'Where is the mother?' signed Derek. Tracey signed, 'Flew away for food.'

Like some giant, jointed animal, the five of us backed out of the den. We smiled broadly at one another.

'All's well that ends well,' said Mr Blick. 'You had better stand guard until we can get a sign made to warn the other children to keep clear,' and off he went. Derek looked at Tracey and tried to make up signs for 'sorry'.

Tracey simply smiled and signed, 'Please listen.' Another phrase which we now knew for the future!

We all nodded to each and took up our stations to guard the nest.

'Funny,' said Derek, 'asking us to listen when there is no sound.'

'That's because she wants us to take notice, instead of just barging in,' added Vinod. Vinod doesn't say much, but when he does it's usually very sensible or he makes us laugh with a good joke.

Follow-up questions

- Why can it sometimes be hard to make others understand what we are trying to say?

- What are the important things to remember when you are really trying to listen to someone else?

Daniel and Koshi

Theme: Daniel's Grandpa has died recently and he really has no idea how to cope, especially as his mum and dad are feeling sad too.

Setting: Buddhist temple

Curriculum reference: Other Religions (Buddhism)

Daniel's Grandpa had died quite recently, and Daniel was missing him terribly. He didn't know what to do with all his love – it kept welling up and overflowing, even through his eyes and nose.

Tomorrow, July 13th, would have been Grandpa's birthday. Daniel was supposed to be going on an end-of-school trip with his class. At first he was excited; his mum let him help choose his packed lunch and join in making it up. His bag was soon full of extra special little treats and some pocket money which he could spend exactly as he wished. But, he suddenly realized, Grandpa usually gave him the pocket money. Immediately, Daniel felt sad and tight in his chest again.

Mum and Dad knew what was wrong. But they had decided that 'least said, soonest mended'.

Next day, Daniel lined up with all the rest of his class waiting to go into the Buddhist temple. They had been learning all about the Buddhist faith at school. Miss Timmins warned everyone to be quiet. 'We must show our respect, when we go into a place that is very special to someone else's belief,' she whispered.

The whole class settled down and filed quietly through the door. Miss Timmins mouthed a huge, 'Well done!', as they passed by.

Once inside, the children marvelled at all the beautiful and exotic statues of the Buddha. Some were made of gold and looked very serene. 'Serene' was a word that Miss Timmins said really described Buddhist monks and, in fact, all the people who followed the Buddhist religion.

'Buddhists take the middle way in life,' Miss Timmins had said. 'They look to harm no living thing. They chant Mantras to help them become kind and wise, and try to be like the Buddha himself.'

A little while later, the monk who was showing them around began to say,

'Today is a special day for Buddhists. July 13th is the beginning of the Feast of Obon, the remembering of our ancestors….' But by then Daniel had stopped listening. He had just spied Koshi's mum, carrying bowls of food into the temple. He remembered her from playgroup, where Koshi had been his very best friend. They had gone to different schools, so they didn't see each other now.

113

What was Koshi's mum doing here, he wondered. But then she disappeared.

The guide was now pointing to some monks making beautiful mandalas, pictures made in coloured sand that represented the Universe.

It was very quiet and peaceful in the temple and Daniel gradually realized that he wasn't feeling sad just at that moment. Even though he had been thinking of Grandpa and how much he had liked his old friend, Koshi, he seemed happier in here.

It wasn't long before Koshi's Mum appeared again. She was now handing out the food to the Temple visitors. It was delicious! Daniel was pleased when she came over and said 'Hello'. He mentioned how much he would like to see Koshi again.

Then Koshi's mum asked him if he would like to come to Koshi's house for a party the next day. 'It's a party for all the family, so you can bring your mum and dad along too,' she added. 'I will ring your mum today and make sure that it's all right.'

'It's not Koshi's birthday, is it?' asked Daniel. 'It would have been my Grandpa's today, but he died.' Koshi's mum smiled. She thought she might be able to help Daniel at this difficult time.

'Oh no, it's Obon we are celebrating – just as the monk was explaining earlier, we will be remembering our ancestors. We do it every year at this time.'

Daniel wished he had listened more carefully.

Back in class, Miss Timmins explained a little more about Obon to the children.

'We were lucky to be in the Temple today,' she said, 'just as they were beginning to celebrate Obon. It's a lovely idea. It's a three-day event, which is similar to a party. On Day One, the Buddhist people invite the spirits of all their relatives back to the home. On Day Two, they have a big party and talk about the wonderful memories they have and, on Day Three, the ancestors and close relatives are sent back to heaven, which is called Nirvana. It is the place they are all trying to reach.'

Daniel began to think. 'What a fantastic idea! A day when he could talk about Grandpa and not worry about upsetting his dad or grandma. A whole day to remember all the good times they had had together.'

'Mum?' asked Daniel on the way home from school. 'Has Koshi's mum rung you yet?'

'She has,' answered Mum, but not very happily.

'Can we go?' asked Daniel.

'Oh, I'm not sure, Dan. It's not so long, since Grandpa died, and I don't want you to get upset all over again. It will bring back lots of memories.'

'I know,' said Daniel. 'But that's why they do it – then they don't forget or feel sad.'

'Oh!' said Mum, sounding a little surprised. She had been trying so hard to not mention Grandpa for fear of upsetting Daniel.

'I really would like to go, Mum. I can tell everyone how fantastic my Grandpa was and tell them about all the things he taught me!'

Mum stopped in her tracks and looked at Daniel.

'You are quite something, Dan. Sometimes you are so grown-up. You put me and Dad to shame.'

'If it's good, Mum,' continued Dan, 'could we do it every year, too? It will be something to look forward to.'

'What a brilliant idea. Come on, let's hurry home and warn Dad and Grandma that we are all off to a very special party tomorrow!'

Follow-up questions

- Why did Daniel think that the party at Obon was such a good idea?
- Can you describe anything about the three days of Obon?

Nisha and the Hare's Fairy

Theme: Buddhists believe in harming no living creature, but Nisha has to be very brave when defending a hare from a group of cruel boys. She is rewarded by being allowed to see the hare's fairy protector.

Setting: Out in the fields

Curriculum reference: Other religions (Buddhism)

Nisha already knew that other people in her village thought she and her family were a bit strange, because they were Buddhist. Other children laughed at her when she begged them not to kill a noisy insect, if it landed on their arms. It was a difficult one, because a gnat annoyed her too, and if it were a mosquito it would surely bite and leave an itchy red lump. But Nisha always tried to be as calm as possible and hope that the insect might fly away, doing her no harm, as she intended it no harm.

Nisha was only six years old and it was hard believing in things that other folk thought odd. But she was a good girl and it never entered her head to simply do as all the other children did. She never joined in when the other children were cruel to one another in words or deeds. She would never think it fun to torment animals.

Consequently, on the day in question, Nisha had to be very brave and think of others and not herself.

Out in the field, a hare had become caught in a horrid home-made trap of string and a wire loop. The hare had been feeding, careless of the danger. He had walked a little too far, close to a bright tuft of yellow daises, when suddenly his front legs felt burning and soon he was in incredible pain. He squealed as only an animal in torment would do. But the more he tried to escape, the tighter the wire cut into his paw.

The noised alerted some boys who came to see what was happening. They teased the hare and, as it tried to get far away from them, it pulled the wire even tighter. Not content with that, one boy found a stick and he was obviously going to hit the hare.

Nisha ran forward.

'NO!' she shouted, as loudly as she could. The sudden noise stopped the boy in his tracks. Nisha stood between him and the wounded hare. She tried to be calm and quiet, as her faith expected her to be. But her heart was pounding with fear and she felt very hot. Nevertheless, she spoke slowly and quietly so that the boys had to listen. 'You must *not* do this. Don't you know how cruel you are being? Can't you see that the hare is in dreadful pain?'

The boys were surprised that such a small child should be so brave. Nisha was spurred on. 'If you tease him any more, he may break his leg as he tries to escape.'

The boys shrugged stupidly. One even began to move forward, as if to try it out. Nisha stood her ground, but she could think of nothing else to say that might stop the boys.

Suddenly a small 'something' with wings fluttered past her face. She didn't try to brush it away – she knew insects were too delicate – one swipe of her small hand could kill it.

Exactly at that moment a thought popped into her head. No sooner did she think it than she said it.

'What if a giant, with huge hands and feet, came through here now and trampled on you – because you were too small and unimportant for him to see? What if you were left with broken bones and bruised bodies? What if you were in pain and needing help? What if no one came, because you didn't matter? How would you like it?'

The boys went white and shuddered at the thought. They were amazed at these words from such a small girl. Slowly they turned and walked away. It seemed as if they didn't care but Nisha knew better. They weren't bad boys, after all.

Next, she knew she had to try and save the hare, but it was too frightened to let her near. He kicked out at her with his

strong, back legs. He tried to nip her with his long, sharp teeth. Nisha was almost in tears. How could she make the hare understand she was only trying to help?

The next thing that happened was so strange that, afterwards, Nisha wasn't really sure that it had actually taken place.

Suddenly it seemed that the winged insect passed in front of her face again. At the same moment, the hare became very still, gazing at the sky. The winged insect now looked more like a fairy to Nisha. It was brightly coloured and rested lightly on the hare's back. Nisha was sure she could see a tiny smile on its face.

The hare looked so peaceful now that she felt brave enough to have another go at releasing the wire. It came away without difficulty. She simply had to ease the string, which then took the pressure off the wire. Then she was able to slip the now large loop over the hare's paw.

She sat very still and watched the hare. He stopped gazing at the sky and closed his eyes. His breathing became much slower and less ragged. After a few minutes, he hopped away, long ears twitching this way and that.

Nisha was about to get up when she noticed the brightly-coloured, winged creature sitting there on her open hand. She was quite sure she heard a tinkling, tiny voice say, 'Thank you, Nisha,' and, with that, it was gone.

Nisha walked home, slowly. No one will believe me, she thought. But later, when she decided to tell her family about her escapade, her great-grandmother nodded knowingly.

'Ah, that will be the hare's fairy – Dana. All creatures have someone looking over them and keeping them safe. It's just that we can't see most of them. Few folk have reported seeing the hare's fairy. You must be a very blessed child, Nisha.'

Nisha wasn't so sure of this. All she had been trying to do was to live up to her beliefs – not only when it was easy, but when it was hard too, like today. Maybe that's why the fairy allowed Nisha to see her.

Follow-up questions

- What brave things did Nisha do to help rescue the hare?
- Why is it important to Buddhists to take care of all living creatures?

The Tigress and the Dragon

Theme: The tigress and the dragon are the faces of yin and yang, the equal and opposites of a balanced person. When they are imbalanced it always leads to trouble.

Setting: China

Curriculum reference: Other religions (Buddhism; Taoism)

Today's story is a Chinese tale about a tigress and a dragon.

The tigress was fearful. She was slinking close to the earth. Her orange, stripy body was camouflaged in the dry grass. She was hunting to feed her cubs. None of them had eaten for four whole days now, and the tigress felt torn between the thrill of the hunt and the terror that she might get hurt, or even die, leaving her cubs all alone. There were also male tigers all around and she knew they would kill her cubs, if they found them. Her head was full of darkness and every muscle was tight with fear. Her ears were flat against her head, but she was listening and watching with every fibre of her body. Everything was her enemy.

The dragon, meanwhile, was sailing through the high sky. He was a beautiful, azure-blue creature, with iridescent sparkles of green and gold. Purple glinted off his magnificent scales. His enormous wings were wide open and flapping lazily, as he gently glided and turned. He rose and rolled in the beautiful Spring morning sunshine. He was pleased with himself. He was the sort of dragon who saw good in everything and everyone. No one was his enemy.

If you like, the tigress was yin and dragon was yang. They could not have been more different.

Sometimes, Tigress Yin wished she could relax and enjoy the warmth of the Sun. But she always had to be on guard, always thinking ahead. She needed to plan and be ready in case of any trouble. Some would say this was a waste of time – worrying about things that might never happen. She was a lonely creature. The other animals avoided her, because she was always in a bad, black mood.

Dragon Yang, on the other hand, never worried. He never planned ahead and never worried about trouble. Sometimes this led him into danger and this always surprised him, because he did not expect it. He had lots of friends, who usually came to help him out. He was never lonely.

Neither creature thought that they could change. They both firmly believed that they were who they were and they would stay that way for ever.

That was until the day of 'Laotzi'. On that very day, they didn't know it, but they were both in the same place, a small farming village in rural China. Tigress Yin was searching for food. Dragon Yang was simply being curious, as he hadn't visited the place before.

The villagers were in uproar. Running from house to house, they were shouting, banging drums, setting off fire-crackers. Mothers were crying and gathering up their children. They were pointing up to the sky then peering into the tall grass on the outskirts of the village.

Yin and Yang could both smell their fear. Yin knew why. In her black mood, she would even be willing to take a villager, if she could catch one, to feed her cubs.

Yang was confused. He couldn't understand what was making them so afraid. He swung in long, lazy circles above the village, getting lower and lower in order to see more clearly. The people became even more afraid.

Then he saw the crouching tigress. He thought he understood their fear. He flew even lower until the villagers could hear the beating of his huge wings and feel the draught they caused.

He tried to scare the tigress away by breathing fire and scorching the grass near her. But that only started a blaze and the wind from his wings blew the fire towards the small wooden huts of the villagers.

Tigress Yin sneered. She would hide from the dragon and wait… wait for one of the villagers to race away from the fire. Then she would have a meal for her family. Her dark heart was laughing at the dragon's mistake.

At that moment, Dragon Yang felt a terrible pain in his shoulder! The people were shooting at him, using arrows and gunpowder sticks.

'Why?' he wondered. He was trying to help them. Again and again, he felt the pains, as more and more of the arrows and gunshot pierced his beautiful, bright, iridescent scales.

He decided it was time to take action. He planned at once to leave and in one smooth, wonderously easy movement he changed direction and flew vertically up into the sky – away from the black smoke and out into the golden sunshine. Safe!

But Tigress Yin had forgotten to plan and take care. Hungry, she still waited and waited… but she waited too long! She felt the great heat of the fire. She was surrounded by burning grass. There was no way to escape. She let out a terrible roar of fear and defeat. The fire consumed her body. Her last black thought was to blame the dragon, as she thought of her cubs, hungry and now in real danger.

That's the end of the story. But Chinese people still believe that we are all made up, half Yin and half Yang, and that each day we must try to balance these two pieces of our character.

The symbol for the yin and the yang are designed to make a perfect circle.

By trying to keep a perfect balance of the two halves of our feelings, Chinese people believe that we can be better, and even the best that we can be.

Follow-up questions

- Why was the dragon surprised when the people started to attack him?
- What was the tigress's big mistake?

Hanukkah Games

Theme: Hayyim is excited because it is Hanukkah and he knows there will be lots of fun and games. Unfortunately he decides to cheat in the game of dreidel, with terrible consequences. He is of course forgiven by his loving family but he has learned a very important lesson.

Setting: Hanukkah celebrations. Big family party

Curriculum reference: Other religions (Judaism)

Hanukkah is a festival from the Jewish Faith and is celebrated in late November and early December. Hayyim, like all the other Jewish people in the world, was looking forward to enjoying this season of fun and games.

Hayyim knew there would be visits to the synagogue. He would get the chance to wear his best clothes and he would hear his favourite story. This told of the return of the Jews to their temple, after the Greek invading army had left. There, they found that all the jars of oil had been lost or broken and that only the tiniest bit of oil was left to fill the temple lamps. In fact, there was only enough to last for one more day. Then the miracle had happened: each day the lamp was lit and each day it continued to shine brightly and the tiny amount of oil actually lasted another eight days, by which time the new supplies had arrived.

Hayyim knew these events had all happened thousands of years ago, but he and the Jewish people still love to remember and to rejoice that their God had sent a miracle to let them know that he was looking after them.

Every Jewish child would receive a present for each day of Hanukkah. The people would eat special food and light lots of lamps to remind themselves of that time, long ago, when God gave them light. The story also helped them to be brave and to stick to their beliefs and values; not letting other folk tell them what to do, especially if they felt that it was a bad thing or something that would make them break a promise.

This year, as always, Hayyim's family was giving parties and special meals, and lots of other family members would be coming to his house to enjoy the eight days of Hanukkah.

Now it was the fourth night of Hanukkah, and all the prayers and blessings had been said and given many times over. Everyone was full of joy. Hayyim's mum had made the house look wonderful with myriads of beautiful lights of all shapes and sizes and colours. Home felt like a magical place. But then everything started to go wrong for Hayyim.

He and his cousins had spent the afternoon playing games, eating sweetmeats and cooking the potato latkes, which was always fun. Hayyim liked to have sweet apple sauce with his, but some of the grown-ups preferred sour cream.

Just then, Isaac, who was fourteen, teased Hayyim about the apple sauce, saying that only little babies chose it. Hayyim became very angry. He sulked and took himself off to a different room to try to cool down. This was a good idea to begin with, except that, before he had time to think, his eyes lit upon the old velvet sack with all the pieces in it for the game of dreidel.

Dreidel is a game of chance and anyone can win, because it all depends where the spinner falls. Hayyim did not understand this properly, but he thought he had found a way to be mean to Isaac, in return for his teasing.

Slowly and carefully, he opened the top of the sack, reached in and took three or four handfuls of the counters that

you had to collect to win the game. He stopped and listened.

He could hear only his own heart beating. He was afraid he would be caught, but even that did not warn him to stop and think about what he was planning to do.

He quickly tightened the neck of the sack and marched back into the room where everyone was enjoying themselves and called out, 'Who wants to have a game of dreidel with me?' Isaac, Daniel and all his cousins thought that this was a good idea. They gathered round and sat in a circle.

'I will give out the counters,' said Hayyim, feeling important and powerful.

'Have you given them all out?' asked Isaac, 'We don't seem to have many tonight.'

'I thought a few less would make the game go quicker,' lied Hayyim, as he placed a few spare counters in the centre of the circle. The others nodded, thinking that would be good idea.

Hayyim felt a twinge in his chest. It felt tight and he had to breathe quickly to get enough air into his lungs.

But the game had begun. The first to twirl the spinner was Daniel. It fell on the symbol for 'nun', which meant, 'do nothing' – neither take from the spare counters in the middle nor give any back.

The next to twirl the spinner was Isaac. The spinner fell on the symbol for 'shin', meaning that he had to put one of his counters back onto the pile in the middle. He groaned, 'Now I won't win.'

Hayyim smiled secretly. His plan was working.

The game continued, one cousin got the 'hey' symbol, 'take half of everything in the centre pile'. Now there were only a few left. Everyone was hoping for the best symbol, 'gimmel', which meant that the player could take everything within the circle.

All through the game, Hayyim had been sneaking a few counters from his pocket and adding them to his pile to make sure he had the most.

Lots of people were 'out' because they had no counters or the spinner kept falling on 'nun' or 'shin'.

At last, it was Hayyim's turn to twirl the spinner again. It fell on 'gimmel'. He took everyone's last counter! He had won!

'YES!' he shouted. 'I've won!' He jumped up and danced around, really pleased with himself that he had beaten Isaac and sealed his revenge.

But as he did so, a few coloured counters spilled from his trouser pocket, cascading all around him and bouncing on the floor. He stopped, dead still and clutched at his pockets, fear in his eyes.

The room went silent. All eyes were on Hayyim.

Then Isaac spoke up, 'I expect the little chap was hiding them away so that none of us would realize how near he was to winning. Isn't that so, Hayyim?'

Quickly, before the tears of shame could fall from Hayyim's eyes, Isaac scooped him up, high in the air, swinging him round and round until his tears turned to laughter.

The prize was a box of pencils that lit up like the Hannukkah candles. There were eight in the box.

'Just enough for me to give one to everyone who played,' said Hayyim.

'But that means you won't get one!' said Daniel.

'That's all right,' said Hayyim, looking at Isaac. 'I won the game, that's enough for me tonight.'

Isaac made the sign for peace and winked at Hayyim. He understood that he too had been wrong in making the others laugh at the young boy.

Follow-up questions

- Why did one careless word from Isaac spoil the whole festival for Hayyim?
- Can you describe what Hanukkah is all about?

Fishing for Tiddlers

Theme: Two sisters growing up in a tiny village in the heart of England, hidebound in the traditions of the farming year and the Church calendar, discover that taking care of each other is an important thing.

Setting: Out in the fields, free as the air, and relying on each other

Curriculum reference: Other religions (Christianity)

Everyone thought that Margaret and Elizabeth (Maggi & Tiz) were twins. Even though Maggi looked more like their dad and Tiz looked like their mum, and even though Maggi was the elder and Tiz was the younger, Maggi was small and Tiz was tall, so everyone thought they were twins.

Maggi and Tiz quite liked keeping up this misconception. It often helped when they were in a scrape, which they often were.

The world had just emerged from World War II and, out in the countryside, it was easy for the rhythm of life simply to return to the Church and the farming seasons' calendar and to continue much as it was before the war.

The major events in the Christian Church, in the village, followed just as surely as Spring followed Winter and the countryside cycle.

Each season of the year held something special for the village to celebrate.

In Winter, there was Christmas and Jesus' birth.

At Easter, in the Spring, Jesus' crucifixion mingled with the joy of Easter eggs and new growth; the birth of little animals and birds and the Resurrection.

At the end of the Summer, the harvest was brought home and celebrated.

Then, in Autumn, there was preparation for All Souls Day – Halloween!

It seemed no time at all from the joys of Christmas to the fun of Spring out in the fields. From the promise of Easter to the plenty of Harvest Festival, from Guy Fawkes' Night and Halloween and back to Christmas again!

Maggi and Tiz hardly noticed the passing of time. You'd think nothing could go wrong. Today, it was Spring again, and they decided to go fishing for tiddlers – little fish that spawned in the local stream, which ran at the bottom of the three fields that separated their village from the next.

They woke early and clammered around for two clean jam jars. They carefully tied string handles around the top to make them easy to carry. Then they spent time hunting busily around to find the shrimping nets from last Summer's holiday at the seaside. Finally, it was time to prepare a packed lunch, and they were off! They would be away, for the best part of a whole day, to 'Skegby Bottoms' as the three fields were known locally. Skegby came from 'Skeg's Byre' when the Vikings had come through and 'Bottoms' meant the lowest end of the village!

The girls had a fabulous day. The gentle Spring sun touched their bare arms and legs. They would have pink stripes above their welly lines and below their t-shirt sleeves when they got home.

Paddling in the brook was cold, but they didn't mind. They were looking for tiny fish, like sticklebacks, or for newts and tadpoles that they would catch and pop in the jam jars, three quarters full of stream water.

The girls would then sit and watch the tiny creatures swimming round and around the jar, before returning them to the stream and setting off themselves for home.

They saw pondskaters and dragonflies and marvelled at their beauty. They felt safe and happy.

Tiz was singing an old hymn, as she was fishing.

'I shall make you fishers of men, fishers of men, fishers of men. I shall make you fishers of men, if you follow me.'

Suddenly Maggi told her to shut up, as she was out of tune. Tiz gave her a push, by way of reply, and by accident Maggi fell into the cold, cold stream. Once she had pulled herself out, she was screaming and coughing all at once and wouldn't stop. Tiz tried to calm her, but she still wouldn't stop.

'Sh! Sh! Sh!' Tiz crooned, stroking Maggi's wet hair. 'You'll soon dry out in the Sun.'

But Maggi kept on crying, because she had hurt her knee really badly on a sharp rock beneath the water and it hurt to put any weight on it.

'Oh, please stop crying,' begged Tiz. But it was impossible, Maggi was in too much pain. 'Shall we go home?' asked Tiz. Maggi cried even louder at the thought of having to hop all the way home on her one good leg.

'Oh, please, Maggi, do stop,' Tiz begged again.

At that moment, she noticed that three very large and curious cows had ambled across to see what all the fuss was about. Maggi saw them too and cried even louder. She was terrified of cows!

Tiz knew that they were in real trouble now. She looked around for help, in any shape or form. Luckily, she heard the village bus trundling down the hill. She ran to the edge of the field and waved her cardigan above her head to attract the driver's attention. Fortunately the bus driver saw her. It was Albert, Gran's cousin, thank goodness!

Albert stopped the bus and clambered down.

'What's the matter, Tiz?'

'Maggi's had an accident and we can't walk home.'

'Not to worry,' said Albert. 'We'll pop her on the bus and as we come back on the next run, we'll drop you both off as we pass your lane.'

'Oh, thank you, Albert,' said Tiz. She ran back to Maggi and, between them, they carried her to the bus.

'What happened?' asked all the old ladies on the bus, who had been to the town to do their shopping. Maggi looked at Tiz and said, 'I slipped on some mud on the stream bank and fell and hurt my knee.'

Tiz looked at her thankfully and promised in her heart not to be so rough next time. Maggi held her hand and whispered. 'It was my fault. You weren't out of tune. I was just fed up with you. You'd been singing the same chorus all day long.' Tiz squeezed her hand. She understood. No need to apologize. The girls smiled at each other.

'Just like twins,' said Mrs Thwaite. 'Looking after each other. Understanding without words being said! Lovely, isn't it!' And all the old ladies on the bus smiled and nodded at the two lovely little girls who were *so kind* to each other.

If only they knew the truth!

Follow-up questions

- Can you name the important events in the Christian calendar?

- Why did Maggi and Tiz have to take special care of each other when they played in the stream?

Salematu's Secret Box

Theme: Salematu is a poor child who has never been to school. She is now ten years old and has just been sponsored to allow her to attend school. She is so happy, despite all the hardships. Her first day at school is a very special one.

Setting: Africa

Curriculum reference: Other religions (Christianity)

Salematu carried the parcel, carefully almost secretly, back to the house where she lived with her father. She knew he wouldn't be there when she got back home. He had set out early that morning to walk the eight miles to the nearest town to look for work. He would spend the whole day there, as he did every day. She knew he would be most unlikely to find any work.

Salematu, however, had just been to school. It was her first day, and she'd loved it. This was the first time she had ever been able to attend. She counted her blessings and decided to say a silent prayer of thanks for the lady in England, who had made it possible for her to go to school in Muwembe.

The long walk to school was six miles there and six miles back, but Salematu wasn't bothered. On the way there, after the first two miles, she had found a friend, Matalebu, and the rest of the journey seemed to fly by. They had chatted and laughed about everything you could possibly think of.

Today was also Salematu's tenth birthday. Normally, such days went unnoticed in her house, especially since her mother had died.

But today Mr N'dabe, who taught all the children together in one large classroom, told everyone it was her special day. He did it for all the children, however old they were.

For at least one day, he made sure that the birthday person felt special. Everyone had to do something for them. It might simply be a kindness or a helping hand, but it really made the day extra special for that child.

Today, the other twelve children in Salematu's class made sure they did kind things for her. Evan had allowed her to use his best crayons to colour her picture. Manderi had shared her lunch. Three of the boys had woven her a mat, from strong bush grass, for her to put by her bed. It was beautiful. The bigger boys had made a see-saw from an old tree trunk and a plank that they had found lying around. Salematu was allowed to choose who should play on it with her.

And finally, Matalebu had spent the lunch-hour braiding her hair into the finest braids she could muster. This meant that Salematu's usually wild, bushy hair swung gracefully to and fro, as she moved her head. It wouldn't last for ever, but it was a labour of love and Salematu was delighted with the results.

The children in the school knew that the people from 'The Church Plan' had been in the village today and all of them were hoping to get a letter from their sponsor. Mr N'dabu usually gave them out at the end of the school day.

Today he was holding a letter and a small parcel and smiling, at Salematu.

She stood stock-still. He beckoned her forward.

'It *is* for you,' he said, still smiling.

How could this day get better?

As he continued handing out the letters to the other children, Matalebu tried to persuade Salematu to open the parcel. But she insisted she was waiting until she got home, savouring the thrill and anticipation.

The school day and the long walk were now over. Finally she crossed the threshold of her home, with her mat and her parcel. She sat on her bed and, with trembling fingers, she carefully opened the layers of the package that had come all the way from England.

Inside there was not only a letter, but a bag and a bright yellow birthday card with a fat little bear on it, carrying a pot of 'Hunny'.

And now she allowed herself to open the bag. Inside she found a beautiful, zipped purse, made from small pieces of felt all sewed together with blanket stitch. The pieces of felt were all different shades of blue, her favourite colour!

As she picked it up, Salematu realized that there was something inside the purse. She shook it gently. It rattled.

She pulled the zip back – only a little too quickly in her excitement – and suddenly the room was full of brightly coloured, rolling beads. Some were round, some were square. Some were tube-shaped and all were different colours of the rainbow. They were scattering and dashing from wall to wall in her small, dried-mud hut.

Salematu simply sat there looking at their myriad colours. She noticed that some were made of painted wood and some were bright plastic, still others were translucent glass. On her lap, where it had fallen, was a glittery piece of golden, threading-string that was still neatly wound.

She began to think of what she might make: perhaps a necklace for her friend Malatebu, a wristband for her father, and surely there would be some left over for her to sort and play with, to make into jewellery in different shapes and patterns, again and again.

Carefully, she collected up her treasure trove and put them all back inside the little felt purse. She clutched it close to her chest and danced around the room, laughing happily.

Salematu would never forget her tenth birthday; a school to attend, a best friend, and a gift from her sponsor. Surely she was the luckiest girl in the whole, wide world.

She pulled out her "secrets" box from under her sleeping roll and put her new treasures inside. Smiling to herself, she began to boil water for her father's evening meal. She wanted to be ready for his arrival home.

What a lot she had to tell him and, who knows, maybe today *would* be the day that her father found work.

Follow-up questions

- Why had the Church been able to help Salamatu?

- Why was going to school so special for Salamatu, despite all the hardship she lived with?

We Three Kings

Theme: Christmas time takes on a whole new look for one little boy who has difficulty understanding the story of the Three Wise Men.

Setting: School and Grandad's house over Christmas

Curriculum reference: Other religions (Christianity)

'So you see,' said Mrs Peak in a really encouraging voice, 'the Gold, Frankincense and Myrrh weren't presents at all, they were simply signposts foretelling what was going to happen in Jesus' life.'

She sat back on the story chair and smiled, breathing out as if she had achieved a 'job-well-done', as she was fond of saying.

Matthew looked down in case she saw the disappointment and complete lack of understanding in his eyes.

At home that evening, Mummy announced that they were going across to Nana and Pops' house. Pops was going to light a real fire in their sitting-room where the children would write their Christmas wish-lists to be sent off to Santa. She was almost as excited as Matthew, Jessie and the new baby, Annie.

It was the same every year, at first you could write down *everything* you wished for, and it didn't matter about spellings or being neat! Then you wrote a neat copy for Santa's old eyes to read easily and only with your five best wishes for him to choose your present from.

Matthew struggled. He puzzled, wrote and crossed out ideas on his list many

times. He was trying to remember what Mrs Peake had said about signposts to mark out his life.

Matthew felt he was a big boy now he was six. Everyone kept telling him how big he was. But, at this moment, he just didn't feel big enough to understand precisely how he was supposed to know what was going to happen to him, when he was a man like Daddy.

In the end, he came up with two ideas. They weren't exactly what he wanted for Christmas, but as Mum and Dad always reminded the children, 'It's not what you *want*, it's what you wish or *hope* for.'

He handed over his rough copy to Dad, who, without even reading it, called to Mum, Nana and Pops. 'Well, Santa's really going to love Matty this year. He only has two wishes!' And he playfully punched Matthew, 'Good lad,' he added.

Matthew smiled, weakly.

Jessie handed over a list as long as her arm, as usual, and then they both set about writing a list for Annie, as she was too small to write her own.

Soon they were in a debate about what Annie wanted.

'I'm sure she would really like an i-pod,' laughed Jessie.

'Oh! How about a remote control all-terraine vehicle?' asked Matthew.

The difference between their silly suggestions was that Matthew's was deadly serious. He had no idea how he could get his hands on one otherwise. Now he had had to learn all the new stuff about Christmas gifts, he had persuaded himself, 'Let's face it, the baby is too small to do anything, let alone play with a favourite new toy. I might as well play with it.'

The fire was blazing up the sitting-room chimney. Everyone was mesmerized by the dancing flames.

'Put the lights out, Pops,' said Nana. 'It's so magical, a real fire.'

The family sat around, using the light from the flames to laugh and talk about Christmases past.

Matthew loved this bit of the ritual, he learned so much about Nana and Pops' childhood. Apparently they *always* had snow for Christmas, when they were small.

Then it was time for the final neat letters to be written, before Pops would quietly read his favourite poem, 'The Night Before Christmas', and then they would all sing as noisily as they could, 'When Santa got stuck up the Chimney!'

Dad called Matthew over to him so that he could help him write his letter. Even though he was six and growing up quickly, Dad still sat him on his knee.

'Now, my little man,' he said. He'd had time to look at Matthew's efforts now.

'This is a strange list. I'm not sure if Santa could get hold of either of these for you in time for Christmas.'

Matthew's eyes were large and sorrowful. 'That's all right, Dad. I'm not really meant to have them till I'm a man, like you.'

'Really?' asked Dad. 'Hmmmm, I'm still not sure about them as presents, even then,' Dad continued. 'I mean, a driving licence and a lottery ticket – what's all that about?'

'Well, if I can drive, when I'm really big, I could become a fireman or an ambulance driver or a policeman and help lots of people, and if I won the lottery I would be rich enough to build lots of hospitals and playgroups and help poorly animals and…'

'Whoa, there!' said Dad, 'they are all amazing ideas, Matt, but what about now, what present would you like to be playing with on Christmas day?'

Matthew looked at his daddy. Dad looked lost and confused, whereas Matthew looked old and wise beyond his years.

'Oh dear, Daddy,' he said, patiently. 'It wasn't presents that Jesus got, you know. It was gifts, and it was those gifts that told us about his future life.' He said it with real conviction, like a man who understands (even though he didn't really!!).

Suddenly the penny dropped and Dad understood.

'Ah! I know what's happened,' he smiled thankfully. 'You've been learning about the Christmas story at school.'

Matthew nodded.

'And Mrs Peake has been trying to explain why a little baby got such grown-up presents or gifts,' he corrected himself, 'when he was born.' Matthew nodded again.

'Well, that's just fine,' Dad almost laughed with relief, but he didn't because he knew Matthew was still deadly serious.

'The good news is, Matthew, that your Christmas list is a wonderful idea – for the future – and I'm so proud of you for thinking so hard about it. But today, I would like to point out a few things. First of all, you're not Jesus and, second, Three Wise Men won't be choosing your gifts or be trying to foretell what you will be when you grow up. Third, you are still a little boy, who *can have* a few presents at Christmas, because your family love you just as you are, right now – six years old and the best boy a family could wish to have.' Then he added, 'Why you're almost a wise man already, thinking about your own future like that!'

Matthew breathed a huge sigh of relief. Dad gave him a big hug.

'What's going on over there?' asked Nana. 'I can't see in the firelight.'

'Just a bit of father and son bonding,' laughed Dad.

He winked at Matty. They both knew it would be their secret.

Dad's heart was full of pride for his little boy. And Matthew's heart was full of love for his wise Daddy.

Annie didn't get a remote control all-terraine vehicle for her first Christmas, but I bet you can guess who did!

Follow-up questions

- What were the three gifts that the Wise Men gave to Jesus?
- What was special about these gifts that made them different from the presents we give today?

Shanaz Takes the Veil

Theme: Shanaz has lived in Britain all her life and has lots of friends, but after a family holiday to India she begins to feel things have changed for her.

Setting: School playground

Curriculum reference: Other religions (Islam)

Shanaz had just come back from a long, long holiday in India. All the family had travelled out together, from where they now lived in England. Once they had arrived there, they had met up with all their relatives, who still lived in her parents' home town in India. It had been one huge party, with lots of sunshine and colour and laughter. Shanaz really hadn't wanted to come back, except perhaps to see her really best friend Elly (one of the 'forever-five-friends') who had made her promise that, on her return, she would tell her everything about the holiday.

During her time in India, Shanaz had become old enough to accept and wear a scarf that covered all her hair. It was a sign that she was growing up. Shanaz was very proud to be seen in her hijab. She felt special and honoured. She and her cousins, who were already old enough to wear the hijab, all helped one other to put their hijabs on in the mornings, before going down to breakfast. It all seemed such fun and quite normal.

The first day back at school in Britain was great. All her old friends rushed over to ask her endless questions about the holiday. The girls also seemed interested in her head-covering. They wanted to know if it meant anything important and if she would ever be seen without it. Shanaz felt special all over again and was proud of her heritage from India.

The second day back at school was not such good fun though.

'Hey, Shaz, 'ave you 'ad your 'ead shaved on your 'oliday?' shouted some of the boys in other classes.

Even Robbie, a good friend before the holiday, was silly and rude. 'Shanaz,' he cried, 'I'm really cold, can I use

your scarf to keep me warm?' And he pretended to shiver and made a grab at her hijab.

Shanaz had promised not to take her hijab off when she was at school and she felt a bit afraid. But she knew Robbie well and decided to call his bluff and not take offence.

'Ooh, Robbie, you'd look like a big girl, if you wore one of these!' she called back. Most of the class laughed with her and she felt she had dealt with that one quite well.

Sadly, it didn't stop there. Things became even more difficult for her as the day progressed. Changing for PE and Games was the first problem. Even her closest friends seemed to get really fed up with her for taking ages to get changed. (But she had to take extra care not to disturb her hijab.)

The next day she didn't go to swimming lessons. This nearly finished everything off for Shanaz.

Returning to school on the swimming bus, the girls had made up a new game which they intended to try out at playtime. They were four of the 'forever' group and they had devised it for just four players, when they were swimming. The moment the bell rang for break, they shot off to play their game, completely forgetting about Shanaz. She was left to wander around the playground alone.

Why were they being like this? It wasn't so long ago that they had all played so well together. They were known as the 'forever-five-friends'. Now it felt as though they would rather be the four friends and forget about Shanaz altogether.

'OK?' asked Mrs Nijjer, the kindest of all the playground supervisors. Shanaz tried to smile and say yes, but it all went wrong and her mouth curled down instead of up. Then tears sprang into her eyes, and suddenly she was sobbing.

'Oh, deary me,' said Mrs Nijjer tenderly. 'Come on now, let's sit here and have a little chat, shall we?' Mrs Nijjer sat quietly and let Shanaz calm down. She waited patiently for her to start speaking.

'I feel silly, it's not really that bad,' mumbled Shanaz. 'It's since I went to India. I felt great there, as though I truly belonged, but now I'm home everything has changed.'

Mrs Nijjer nodded and agreed occasionally, but she let Shanaz talk all her feelings out.

'It was lovely to be like everyone else in India,' said Shanaz. 'But now I'm home, it's making me different and I feel I don't belong here any more. I've known my friends since the first day we all started playgroup together. They know I've lived here all my life.' Shanaz sniffed and, when she paused to blow her nose, Mrs Nijjer decided to put a thought into Shanez's head.

'Do you remember when Lizzie in your class had nits and her mum cut off nearly all her hair? Lizzie was able to ignore everyone's teasing and didn't worry about suddenly being different. And then there was that time that Molly's mum let Molly have her nose pierced and everyone asked stupid questions about how she could possibly blow her nose?'

Shanaz looked up, her large beautiful eyes still full of tears. 'Yes, but Lizzie's hair grew a little day by day and Molly doesn't wear her nose piercing all the time. I will always have to wear my hijab. They think I've changed, that I am different because of it, but I made a promise and I must keep it.'

'You think they will never stop teasing you, but you know they stopped teasing Lizzie when her hair was still really short and they don't even think about Molly's piercing any more, whether she has it in or not,' Mrs Nijjer added.

'Maybe you should take some time in Special Assembly to explain to the class how important it is to you to know about your culture and to be part of it. Try to remember how proud you felt in India. The important thing is, that this is you now, this is who you are.'

Shanaz smiled. She was remembering the Sun on her face in India, the laughter of her cousins and then she realized that the Sun had come out here in the playground and that the laughter she could hear was that of her friends nearby.

In fact, Elly was calling her. 'Come on, Shanaz, we need you to help us. We want to know if the game works with odd, as well as even, numbers!'

Shanaz jumped up and started towards her friends. But suddenly she paused and turned back to Mrs Nijjer. 'Thank you,' she said, with a big smile on her face.

Mrs Nijjer nodded and smiled back. She knew that Shanaz had realized that it doesn't matter how much we change our outward appearance, true friends still only see the real you.

Follow-up questions

- Why did Shanaz feel more at home in India than when she came home again?
- What was the important lesson that Shanaz learnt from talking to Mrs Nijjer?

Evacuation

Theme: Two little boys are sent from the war-torn streets of London to a village in Wales for the duration of World War II. They have no idea what to expect and are very nervous about what will become of them.

Setting: At home in the East End and in the tiny Welsh Community Hall

SEAL reference: New beginnings; **Curriculum reference:** Humanities (World War II)

Harold and Morris were two scruffy little kids from the East End of London. They shared a big brass bed with two other brothers. All four had overcoats across the bed to keep them warm. Every night during 'the Blitz', they listened to the drone of aeroplanes overhead.

'Shelter!' screeched Mam, from the bottom of the stairs. The two bigger lads dragged the smaller boys from the bed and they all dashed for the Anderson shelter at the bottom of the garden.

Morris was whinging even before they were all out of bed. He hated it. They all did.

'But it's better'n being flattened to death when the 'ouse gets bombed and falls on your 'ead,' rattled Mam, and she clouted him round the ear with the back of her hand, just for good measure.

'I wish I never 'ad to live in London,' cried Morris. His mum and dad looked across the gap at each other.

'What?' asked Harold, glaring at Mam. He was a bright lad and he knew that look.

'Nuffin',' said Mam. 'Get some sleep or you won't get up in the mornin'.'

'There's nuffin' to get up for,' said Harold. 'They bombed our school last week remember?' His parents shared that look again.

'Well, we'll just 'ave to wait 'n see, shan't we!' grumbled Mam. Harold thought she was going to cry. He turned over on his bunk, but he didn't sleep. Something was going to happen tomorrow, he just knew it, and it wasn't going to be good.

He was right. Next morning, they had a slap-up breakfast. 'Ate nearly everythin' in the 'ouse!' his brother said later. Then Mam got them dressed up in their Sunday best clothes.

'Where we goin', Mam?' asked Morris. 'It's not Sunday today!'

'No, Love,' she said, blowing her nose, hard into her hanky. 'I'll tell you all later.'

Next she led them to the train station. Mr Wicks, the Headmaster, and Mr Graham, their Class Teacher, and all the other teachers, were there to meet them.

'Line up Class 2,' shouted Mr Graham, like some bossy Sergeant Major. 'Line up – alphabetical order please!'

All the children, from each Class of Plaistow Infants, did as they were told.

Luckily there were only 10 months in age between Morris and Harold, so they were both in the same class.

'Find a partner next to you and hold hands,' Mr Graham shouted again. The boys hung on grimly to each other.

Next, the Headmaster walked down the lines with a stern look on his face. He was checking that every child had a gas-mask box and a bag or case, in which should be three changes of clothes.

Mam only had a brown-paper carrier bag and one string bag. Harold had the carrier bag, which meant that Morris's few vests, pants, spare trousers, one extra shirt and a jumper were all bulging out of the holes in the string bag, for all to see. A boy, with a small brown leather suitcase, pointed this out and laughed at Morris's poverty. Mr Wickes glared at him and he blushed bright red and turned away.

Morris was still holding tightly on to Mam's hand, as well as to Harold's. 'Let go now, Darlin',' she begged. He held on even tighter. 'Nah! Mate, let go. Yer dad and I 'ave to get off, nah.' She was definitely crying.

'What's 'appenin', Ma?' asked Harold.

'It's the evacuation,' said Dad, as though it explained everything.

'You're goin' to the country to be safe, 'til the war's over,' he added.

Morris began to blubber.

'Now stop that young Morris Andlaw – it's not your mum or dad's fault, it's the government who are organizing this trip,' bawled Mr Wicks, from the front of the line.

Morris stopped. 'Trip?'. He knew that word. He'd been on day trips to the seaside, that was okay, it meant they'd be back tonight.

No one told him otherwise.

He cheered up, kissed Mam and Dad and hopped onto the train, that was hissing and steaming like a great beast straining to leave the station.

Several hours later, in the dark and cold, they all walked from Llangadog station to the village hall. Inside, it was all bright lights and steamy cold breath. There were lots of local people grouped around the edges, all staring at the 'waifs from London'.

A bossy lady with a clipboard, and an accent they could hardly recognize, began calling their names and offering the children to these local people, as if they were at a cattle-market, buying sheep or cows.

'Morris and Harold Andlaw, brothers, both six years old, not twins, need to stay together,' called the woman. 'Mr Davies, any good to you on the farm?'

'Too small!' he shouted back.

Morris wanted to cry, but Harold was squeezing his hand really hard and the pain took his mind off it.

After that, three other sets of people had said 'No' to the boys. Harold and Morris began to feel worthless. Their heads bowed and they stood as close together as was possible, each taking comfort from the other.

'Mrs James!' called an old grizzly-bearded man from the back of the crowd. 'I'll have those boys. I could use a couple of 'titches' to go up the chimneys!' He laughed, and everyone joined in. The boys didn't know if it was a joke or not.

Both cried quietly all the way to his farm, as they travelled in the pony and trap. They were shivering and scared. What was waiting for them?

BUT, when they arrived, they walked into an amazing room. There was the smell of cakes baking, a huge fire roaring up the chimney, a table spread with a feast, hot tea being poured and pyjamas warming on the range.

The grizzly man smiled at his dear wife. 'Here you are, my love,' he said, gently pushing the two lads forward. 'The family we were never blessed with.'

Mrs Evans held out her arms and cried tears of joy. For these two boys, at least, evacuation was going to be a fine experience.

Follow-up questions

- What was the 'evacuation'?
- Why did the Government take this action during the Blitz?

Who's to Blame?

Theme: Grace goes into service when she is seven and it is far from what she expected. All the girls are tired and this leads to a dreadful accident. Grace's forgiveness seals a friendship for life.

Setting: The scullery in a big house

Curriculum reference: Humanities (Victorians)

In the grand Victorian house, where she worked as a maid, Grace was 'poshing' away in the dolly tub and she was exhausted. The tub was made of wood and it leaked. Her shoes and feet were alternately freezing from the cold slate floor or boiled by the water coming from the tub. Grace's arms ached so much, she was sure that she could hear them creaking.

The 'dolly' that Grace had to hold tightly and twist around energetically from side to side to clean the clothes, felt heavier and heavier.

This was Monday's job for Grace. The master's white cotton clothes had been soaked overnight to help soften the stains, then they were boiled first thing on Monday morning. Finally, Grace had to push and pull the dolly, until the cottons were spotless – nothing less would do. Grace could have cried with the effort. She had to get up at 4 am every washday to begin this routine.

Grace was seven years old when she had had to leave home and 'go into service', as they called it. She missed her ma and all her brothers and sisters (16 babies: nine boys and seven girls, including Grace). Thirteen had survived their first year, but now, since the influenza outbreak that winter, there were only eleven of them left.

Grace had been excited about going into service. Her older sisters had gone before her and they all sent money home to make life easier for Ma. Grace imagined she would enjoy being a worker after her seventh birthday.

None of her sisters had told her how lonely she would be, or how cold it would be, that first long winter on her straw bed in the attic, with only one blanket that scratched her skin.

None of them had told her how badly her hands would blister and bleed from

chillblains. Sometimes she could hardly bend her fingers when she woke up to begin work.

None of them had told her what the days would be like. 'The days are as long as they need to be to do all the work!' Mrs Crawley, the housekeeper, was fond of telling Grace and the other scullery maids.

Grace's name might imply that she was a gentle girl full of kindness. But this was not so. She had a fiery temper and often said what she thought without thinking of others' feelings first. Ma had warned her to curb her temper or she would lose her job for sure, and the family needed the money to survive. Grace had taken her words to heart.

Grace gazed at the murky water in the dolly tub. She thought she was probably pushing more dirt in than squeezing it out.

'More hot water!' she shouted to Winnie.

'You just 'ad some!' Winnie yelled back.

And, just for spite, Winnie took the boiling pan off the copper and poured it from a great height into the tub. The water fell like a thundering waterfall. It splashed off the clothes, drenching Grace in scalding water.

There was silence for a few seconds, as Winnie realized what she had done and as Grace, momentarily, did not feel the pain. Then the scream she let out reverberated across the yard. It travelled from the scullery to the kitchen, to the sheds where the animals were, to the vegetable gardens where the boys

worked, and even up to the mistress's sitting room!

Everyone ran towards the heart-rending cries. Except the mistress. She rang her dainty bell, summoning her personal maid, so that she might ask who on Earth was making such a dreadful noise when she was trying to have her nap!

The sight that met their eyes, when everyone crowded into the washhouse, was pitiful. Grace looked so small and frightened. Her face was white as snow and where the water had caught her skin she was as red as Christmas berries.

All of them began shouting orders and helpful hints.

'Fetch the butter and smother her in it,' called Old Peggy.

'No,' screeched Miriam, a downstairs maid. 'Cover her in wet cloths to keep the air out.'

'NO!' commanded Mrs Crawley. Everyone stopped and stepped back from Grace. The little girl looked terrified and was crying like a little lamb who needed its mother.

'Geoff, get that lid off the cold copper outside. Frank, lay her carefully on top, then both of you carry her to the stream in the low field and hold her body under the water for a slow count of at least 100.'

Everyone moved away. The boys did not question Mrs Crawley. Quickly and efficiently, they carried the trembling Grace down to the stream.

'I can't swim,' she stammered, shivering with shock.

'You won't have to. It's not very deep – just very cold,' said Geoff.

Within minutes Grace was lying in the stream and the cool waters were taking the heat and sting out of her burning skin.

She smiled bravely at Geoff, and at Winnie, who had followed them.

'Don't worry,' she said. 'I'll be all right. It's so nice in here. I feel like a water baby.'

Winnie gave a weak smile in return and mouthed silently, 'I'm sorry.'

Grace nodded; she understood. They were all tired and short-tempered on washday. Winnie hadn't planned to scald her, but she knew she had thrown the water too hard and was now feeling guilty about the consequences of her actions.

'It's one accident too many,' complained Mrs Crawley. 'And believe you me, when her ladyship asks me what and why and who's to blame, I'll be telling her the truth. We need more girls in the scullery, I shall say, so that it's not such a panic from dawn to dusk every Monday!'

Things changed in the big house after that. Grace's scalds healed. Even before she went home on Mothering Sunday (the only day in any year she had off to visit her family), you could hardly see the scars.

Winnic and Grace became firm friends and years later Winnie said, 'I'm so glad you didn't blame me after the accident, Grace. You'll never know 'ow sorry I was.'

'I do,' answered Grace. 'But my ma always taught us to never assume the worst in others. It's so easy to blame and much harder to put yourself in their shoes, but it does work.'

Follow-up questions

- Did Winnie mean to harm Grace by pouring the water too quickly?

- Why did jobs in the home take so much longer in Victorian times?

Wanted – a Friend

Theme: Two very different children are feeling pretty lonely, quite by accident, they both go to the same place, though for very different reasons. There they discover that they have a lot in common.

Setting: Britain during the Roman settlement

SEAL reference: Relationships;

Curriculum reference: Humanies (Romans)

Janus was the son of a Roman Officer sent over to Britain during their occupation of the country in 55 BC. Janus was very lonely, since not many of the soldiers were of a high enough rank to be allowed to bring their families with them to Britain. Janus wasn't happy in this cold new land.

Boudicca was the daughter of an Elder of the Icene Tribe. But Boudicca didn't look like a princess. She was most often to be found covered in dirt with her hair wild and straggly, and with great tears in her clothes. Life in Britain at that time was very different now that the Romans had come. Boudicca wasn't happy that the Romans were in Britain.

One bright, but bitterly cold, day, Janus decided to go hunting for birds' eggs to keep himself warm. By climbing up the very steep hill behind the encampment, he was sure he would find the nest of that huge bird he had seen flying around.

And so it was that twenty minutes later, out of breath but warm as toast, he was lying face to the ground, looking straight into the eyes of a Peregrine Falcon. He was so close, he realized that he was holding his breath in fear of disturbing this amazing creature.

The Peregrine Falcon was absolutely still. Its wings were spread wide over the prey it had just caught and that it was still holding tight in its talons. Janus knew that the bird was staring straight back at him. He closed his eyes, frightened that the bird might attack him. Suddenly the bird took off. A great, downward draught whooshed across Janus's face, lifting his fringe. He peeped out and saw the bird soaring away higher and higher, with the rabbit still in its claws. He checked to make sure that it landed on top of an over-hanging crag. He realised that that must be where the nest was and decided to climb up to see if there were any eggs.

It was a very difficult climb. Soon he was covered in little cuts and bruises, plus he had torn his tunic, which would mean trouble when he got home. But Janus wasn't bothered; this was the best fun he had had, ever since they had landed on this cold unpleasant little island.

Unknown to Janus, Boudicca was also climbing the cliff face today to check on the state of the chicks and make sure the Peregrine Falcon had not been disturbed. Both children had been lying hidden in the rough grass and bracken but on different sides of the crag. They each had a good view of the eyrie and could see the magnificent female falcon tearing up the prey and feeding it to the largest chick. The second chick was still quite wobbly and found it difficult to push to the front to get some of the meat.

On a previous visit, Boudicca had counted two more eggs that had not yet hatched. At least, for now, there were fewer nestlings to fight for any food the mother could provide.

Both children realized that they would have to wait for the mother to go off hunting again before they could make a move – Boudicca because she didn't want to disturb the new family and Janus for his chance to steal one of the eggs.

Suddenly Janus lost his footing and began to slip down the hillside. He called out in fear and surprise. This attracted the feeding mother and in a flash she flew at Janus, screeching and flapping her huge, powerful wings. As the falcon rose, she pushed her long talons forward to attack the enemy that she thought was after her chicks. There was a scream as she caught Janus with a slash of her claws across his face.

Immediately, Boudicca leapt up from her hiding place. Brandishing a big stick, she bravely rushed in and tried to frighten the bird away. Although the bird was brave, it knew it couldn't fight off two enemies at once, so it flew up and away. The children ran off down the hill tumbling and rolling in their panic in case the bird might return.

Eventually they came to rest among the grass and rocks. They lay panting and sobbing and still afraid. Boudicca turned and saw blood on Janus' face. Luckily, they were close to an ice-cold stream, Boudicca took some moss and soaked it in the cool water and went to bathe his face. As Janus pulled away, they realized that they did not speak each others' language.

Boudicca looked at Janus and mimed that she only wanted to help. He nodded and let her put the cool clean water over the wound. It was so cold it seemed to freeze the pain away. Janus smiled and said thank you. Boudicca didn't understand his words, but she knew what they meant and smiled back at him.

As they walked back to the camp, they chatted using signs or pictures drawn in the soil. Sometimes they spoke to each other in their own language, very simply, and pointing to each object. One way or another, they managed to become instant friends.

The two remained good friends for many years. Boudicca often painted a scar on her face to look like the one on Janus's. They were a gang of two against the world. Janus often laughed to think how far he had had to travel to find his very best friend, and Boudicca laughed, because she had only ever wanted to be a warrior, and now she had finally found a boy who believed she was!

Little did they know, that thousands of years later, people would remember her as the famous warrior, Queen Boudicca, for the way she had fought to save her family, her people and her country – just like she had when she bravely defended Janus against the bird.

Follow-up questions

- What things did Janus and Boudicca have in common?
- In what ways did Boudicca show herself to be brave?

Orange Smarties

Theme: Owen gets himself into a real dilemma when he assumes that what happens in his house with all the orange Smarties is the same as at his friend Arjen's house. (Mamgu pronounced Mamgi)

Setting: Visiting a friend's house for tea

Curriculum reference: Science (some things that look like sweeties are in fact *not* sweeties and are therefore not good for us. Some good drugs that doctors give to people to help them get better can look like sweets).

Owen's Mamgu (Welsh for Grandma) loved orange Smarties. She said they were the best, the only ones with any real flavour. Consequently Owen and his brother always saved them for her. Mum collected them in a little glass jar that had a rubber lid to keep them safe and to make sure all the flavour stayed in.

Mamgu was always delighted when they turned up with a full jar. And even better, she always shared them with Owen and Dafydd.

Owen was a good boy, who could be trusted to be kind at all times. So when Arjen came to their school and the Teacher asked Owen to be Arjen's 'school-buddy' for the first week, she knew she had made a good choice. She knew Owen could be trusted to tell Arjen everything there was to know about their school.

Arjen and Owen got on really well straightaway and almost before the week was over they had become best friends.

Arjen went to Owen's house for tea after school. Owen went to Arjen's house to play and soon their mummies became good friends too!

One day, Owen went to the bathroom at Arjen's house. He had just washed his hands for tea, when he saw a glass jar with a tight lid, full of orange Smarties!

'What are they doing in the bathroom?' thought Owen. 'Wow! There must be hundreds in there. Arjen's grandma must really like orange Smarties too.'

He tried to count them roughly, but as he was twirling the jar around, he found

out that the lid was not on tight at all. It fell off and all the 'Smarties' poured over the tiles on the bathroom floor.

'Oh! no!' he shouted. No one heard. He fell onto his knees and began gathering them up, and putting them back into the bottle, but they kept missing and rolling away again. It was very annoying.

'Go in!' he said. 'Go in!'

After what seemed like ages, most of them were back in the glass jar. Owen had seven or eight in his hand. He looked guiltily over his shoulder as if someone might be watching him.

'Who would notice?' he thought. 'Arjen's grandma can't know how many Arjen has collected for her – just a few less won't hurt.' He looked at them in his hand for a long time, but he felt so naughty that he eventually put them all back in the jar. A couple rolled away, but he didn't care. He just wanted to get out of the bathroom.

Owen quickly screwed the lid down and carefully placed the jar back on the shelf. His hands were shaking. He washed the orange stains from off his hands and went to dry them. He found that his hands were shaking so much, he couldn't grip the towel.

'It's because I was nearly a thief,' he thought. 'I've been wicked and I'm scared someone will know.'

He wanted to cry, but he didn't. He knew he had to look normal or they would start to ask questions.

Back at the tea table, Owen began to feel sick, through worry. 'Is this what happens when you nearly steal something?' he wondered.

'Are you alright, Owen?' asked Arjen's mummy.

'Uh-huh,' mumbled Owen. In fact he was feeling far from alright.

'You look a bit pale,' she said.

'I'm alright really.' He tried to smile, but his face felt stiff and wouldn't work. He began to feel a bit dizzy now.

Just then Arjen came down from washing his hands. 'Mummy, I've just found some of Grandma's tablets on the bathroom floor.'

Owen knew straightaway that he had to own up. He felt so much better after he had told them all the truth. 'I thought they were orange Smarties,' he finished.

But still both mummies sounded really concerned. 'You didn't eat any of the tablets, did you?' they kept asking. And he assured them, he had not.

'I really don't know why Grandma left them on the shelf, with the lid loose,' said Arjen's mummy. 'She is usually so careful to put them well out of reach, especially with Arjen being so young. She must have been in a hurry.'

When they were sure that Owen was okay, the two mummies chatted with the boys. 'You see we all did something wrong,' said Owen's mummy. 'I hadn't warned Owen about the difference between tablets and sweets. Arjen's grandma didn't know the boys were going to play and to be extra careful with her medication today, and Owen shouldn't have taken anything that was not his – especially as they were most certainly were *not* sweets.'

'Let's just be really thankful that nothing terrible has happened,' said Arjen's mummy. 'You do feel alright now, don't you?' she added, looking at Owen.

'I feel fine, and I'm glad I know the difference between tablets and sweets now. And I know *never* to take anything that's not mine,' answered Owen, 'Whatever I think they are!'

'Can we have some tea, now?' asked Arjen.

Follow-up questions

- Why is it important to recognize the differences and dangers between sweets and tablets?

- What could have happened to Owen, if he had swallowed the tablets?

The Purple Pansy

Theme: Nature in all its predatory glory. Mr Fox thinks he is the last in the chain until the day that 'man' steps in and for no good reason manifests himself as the highest in the food chain.

Setting: The flower border

Curriculum reference: Science (food-chains)

Purple Pansy nodded her head in the spring breeze to her friend, Yellow Pansy, across the border.

'How are your leaves, Yellow? Any slug damage last night?'

'You bet!' moaned Yellow Pansy. 'Why is it that the honey-bee comes and fills his sacks with my pollen and drinks my nectar and I hardly notice him at all, but those darn slugs cause so much trouble!'

'I know,' replied Purple Pansy. 'They creep up in the night, slip-sliding all over our leaves and scraping their rough tongues over them. It's just not good enough. My Percy says there should be a law against them!'

'Well, I suppose there is, in a way. Mr Blackbird enjoys a good slug or two for his breakfast. I've noticed that the slugs soon scarper when dawn breaks and the birds come out.'

Meanwhile, at home in the slugs' daytime hiding place, Mrs Slug was looking worried. Mr Slug wasn't home yet and the Sun was already getting high in the sky. Her antennae stalks popped in and out in a most agitated manner.

'Shall we go and look for him, Mum?' asked several of her offspring.

'No, no!' she wailed. 'I don't want that dratted blackbird eating you too.'

'You don't know he's been gobbled up. Maybe he's paused to pass the time of day with Walter Worm. He often does,' said Sidney.

Away in Blackbird's nest, the new chicks had sensed Dad was back. They opened their brilliant, red mouths, edged in bright yellow to make them really visible. Their scrawny little necks wobbled under the weight of their huge heads and beaks. They twittered and twittered.

Blackbird regurgitated the food he had just eaten into the seven red caverns, and the frantic twittering stopped.

'Good job I caught two slugs today, Mother,' he whistled gaily. 'Otherwise this lot would run me ragged.'

'Well done, Boris', she whistled back. 'But don't get too brave, I noticed Ginger Tom-cat, skulking around in the shrubbery this morning. Make sure you don't become his breakfast!' Blackbird bobbed up and down on his stick-like legs and flew off to look for more food.

Ginger Tom-cat was playing happily on the step to the kitchen door. It wasn't Boris he had caught, it was another bird, a small robin. It was already dead, but Ginger Tom-cat liked to feel powerful and had used it as a game for a while before he gobbled it up.

'Uggh!' protested Bessy, a little girl who lived in the house. 'You miserable moggy – you weren't even that hungry. You'd better watch out that Wild Dog Fox doesn't gobble you up. He has cubs to feed you know.'

But Fox was already back in his den feeding his mate, who in turn was feeding the tiny cubs. They were so new that even their eyes weren't open yet.

'I'm glad you went for a rabbit and not fat Ginger Tom-cat. I think he might have put up quite a fight,' said Mrs Fox.

'Don't you worry about me,' boasted Dog Fox. 'I'm the top of the food chain around here!' And off he ran, quick as a streak of lightning, across the morning fields, hoping for one more kill, before the day got too hot and filled with humans.

All the creatures heard the bang! Some even saw, with their sharp beady eyes,

the flash as the gun discharged its bullet. But only the man saw Dog Fox, lying still in the middle of the field.

'Should have stuck to the hedgerow,' said the poacher. 'I'd not have noticed him if he'd stayed in the undergrowth.'

'Aye aye,' agreed his poacher mate, 'pride often goes before a fall.'

They nodded together, feeling pleased with themselves, but they were actually no better than Ginger Tom-cat. They had killed just for the fun of it. All they had wanted was to practise shooting. They had no intention of sustaining their families with a meal of fox meat! They simply left the dead fox out in the sun for carrion birds to peck at.

Follow-up questions

- Can you describe the order of the food chain in this story?

- Why were Ginger Tom-cat and the poachers the odd ones out in the food-chain?

Mum Knows Best

Theme: Small boy thinks he can outwit his mum and sneakily tries to get the sweet treats he thinks he ought to be able to have.

Setting: At home. After Sunday lunch

Curriculum reference: Science (healthy eating)

'Your trouble is, you don't even know when you are full!' moaned Mum.

Lal prowled round the kitchen, looking for something to eat less than twenty minutes after finishing off a three-course Sunday lunch! He was cross; ever since Mum had become hooked on the 'Healthy Eating for all the Family Plan', which she had picked up on their last trip to the Doctor's surgery, there were no biscuits, crisps, chocolate or cakes left in the house!

'Empty calories,' called Mum, as she went upstairs for a shower. 'There's a lovely juicy green apple in the fridge. Eat that, if you must!'

Lal did not want an apple, he wanted something sweet!

Lal looked like a caged, wild animal, as he checked and re-checked the cupboards in the kitchen. Round and round he went. Round and round, opening and closing the same cupboard doors. He even began to take out anything that looked vaguely as if it might be suitable: cocoa powder, icing sugar, a tin of raspberries, food colouring, raisins; he even found an ancient packet of Instant Pudding powder!

Lal looked at them all laid out on the table. 'I'll show, Mum!' he thought. 'I will cook myself a cake to nibble on!'

As Lal began stirring all the ingredients together, he realized that he needed more 'wetness' to help it bind together. Then with great difficulty, he managed to carry the large mixing bowl to the sink and balance it under the tap. He turned the water on a little too forcefully and most of it bounced out of the bowl, taking quite a lot of the mixture with it, ending up with it spread all over the floor.

'That will just have to do,' he thought and, with a mighty effort, he poured the mixture into a tin.

Oh, yes! He needed to put hundreds and thousands on the top. He lifted out the tub, thinking he knew what he was doing, but its label was worn and difficult to read. Even so, he opened the lid and shook the pot violently over the mixture.

Surprisingly, myriads of tiny coloured balls didn't flood onto his cake mix, but instead a puff of fine white powder flew out and floated around making him sneeze and covering everything around in a fine white layer.

149

Immediately the mix went crazy – bubbling and frothing like a mad dog. Lal knew straightaway something was wrong.

His 'cake' got bigger and bigger in the tin.

Thinking quickly, Lal dashed it to the oven, slid it inside and slammed the door shut!

He then turned a few of the dials as he had often seen his Mum do before. Then he stood back, feeling mighty pleased with himself.

'Job done. Easy!' he thought.

He wiped his hands on his T-shirt and, ignoring the mess he had made, went off to ride his bicycle.

Once busy playing, Lal forgot completely that he had been feeling hungry. He called at Arthur's house and played there for a while. That was until, he heard the *call*! Well actually

most of the street must have heard the call, because it was really more of a bellow.

'Lal!' It was Mum. 'Lal, back home, NOW!'

This did not sound good.

Mum virtually dragged him into the house. He could smell a strange, burning smell as they got nearer the kitchen.

Mum opened the door on a scene of 'epic mess' proportions.

'Oops,' said Lal, quietly.

Gunge was drooling out of the oven. Slippy, slimey stuff covered the floor. The table top was covered in a mountain of the dregs of everything that he had used.

'Clear it all up. But don't touch the oven,' growled Mum, through gritted teeth.

It took ages.

No one came to help.

When he had finished and was thinking that he had made a good job of it, Mum appeared.

'Finished yet?'

'I think so,' said Lal, looking forlornly at the floor.

'Good, it's tea-time.' said Mum, and she carefully opened the oven door and took out what can only be described as a dinosaur-droppings cake!

'You're having cake for tea!' she announced and began scooping out huge lumps of the dollopy gunge onto a plate.

'Enjoy!' she smiled and waited.

Lal looked a little green around the gills.

'I don't actually feel hungry,' he mumbled.

Mum took a lovely juicy apple from her pocket. 'Could you eat this?' she asked more kindly.

Lal smiled, as he took the apple. 'Sorry, Mum.'

Mum smiled back.

'Always remember, Lal, Mum knows best, and don't *ever* mess up my kitchen again!'

Follow-up questions

- Do you think Lal really was still hungry after his Sunday lunch?
- What mix of foods help us to get a balanced diet?

The Sunflower Seed

Theme: Patience has never been Jessie's strong point, but now she needs it in abundance. She manages to convince herself that she has killed her seedlings before they have even burst through the soil. Mr Wood saves the day with a few wise words.
Setting: Classroom science lesson
SEAL reference: Going for goals; **Curriculum reference:** Science (plants)

Jessie hadn't been in 'big school' very long, but she really enjoyed it. Christmas had been such fun, especially with the play and the party. Class 1 had really enjoyed themselves.

Now it was a new year and a new term. Jessie was excited. Mr Wood was going to take them for science this afternoon. He wasn't a teacher, but he helped the school with their garden and allotment. He had even persuaded Mrs Gittings, the Headteacher, to allow him to put a hen-house on the allotment and the children were hoping for eggs and chicks.

But today, he was coming in to help with 'growing things'.

After lunch, their teacher got them ready. She had covered their tables with lovely clean washable PVC covers.

'You won't need any pencils, rubbers or rulers,' she said, 'just your hands and whatever Mr Wood gives you.'

The whole class sat expectantly, looking at the towers of biodegradable pots, the wild colours of the compost bags, the smaller packets of seeds and the trowels, the jugs of water and the lolly sticks. Jessie reckoned there was enough of everything for them all to have one each. Great! She loved having all her own kit.

Sharing was tough and she was still trying to get better at waiting her turn.

Waiting was so difficult for Jessie, especially when Tony jumped in, whenever he felt like it, and never waited. If you tried to explain to him that it wasn't his turn, he was just as likely to wallop you with whatever he had taken! Jessie knew she felt sorry for him. He was obviously finding it even more difficult then she was, but forgiving was hard too.

There was a little ripple of excitement as the class saw Mr Wood, walking past the window. It brought Jessie back to the present.

Everyone sat up straight, wanting to be good for him. He was such fun. You learned so much without even realizing it, when Mr Wood came into class.

'Now just before we start,' said Mr Wood. 'You'll probably think I'm a daft old man to mention it, but you must remember to talk to your seeds and plants as they grow. They really do need a bit of encouragement, just like you children do,' he laughed.

'I've given you a few seeds each, because we can't guarantee that they will all germinate,' explained Mr Wood.

'This way we can be extra sure that all of you will get at least one lovely big sunflower to enter into the competition.'

'Competition?' they all chorused.

'Oh, I forgot to tell you. There's a prize for the tallest plant, to be judged on the Friday before the Summer term ends.' He gave the thumbs up sign and smiled a big smile at them all. 'Off you go!' he called out.

But Jessie was worried and slowly took care with everything she did. She had already named her seeds and she didn't want any of them to fail – not now she knew them by name!

After she had half filled her pot with compost and dampened it carefully with some water, she laid her seeds in the shape of a square in the compost.

She found a crayon on the floor and quickly drew a diagram of what her pot looked like – each seed with its name beside it – Molly, Sam, Jessie and Fred. All her family: Mum, Dad, herself and her new baby brother. Then she put a small yellow dot on the front of the pot so she would know which way should face the front when she checked how each of them was doing.

Finally she carefully covered them with more compost, dampened it with more water, wrote her name on her lolly stick and stuck it into the pot .

'Now, everyone, listen,' said Mr Wood.

'Keep them damp, give them lots of sunlight and don't put them outside until it gets warmer. Remember to speak to them often, especially once they have grown up out of the soil, and all will be well.'

'Thank you, Mr Wood,' said the teacher, 'we are all very pleased with our science class today. Right, table monitors collect up the spare equipment and put it away.'

While everyone busied themselves clearing up, Jessie put her seed pot at the back of the classroom with all the others, and she prepared to wait.

Two weeks later, nearly everyone had signs of one or two seedlings coming up through the compost. But not Jessie. She began to worry all over again. As others grew strong and tall, she worried even more. Soon some needed a small stick to support them as they grew even taller, Jessie became concerned.

Next day she sneaked into class early and talked to her pot. She explained all her worries to her seeds. She said sorry in case she had set them too deep, sorry in case they were too wet, sorry in case they were too dry. Indeed she was sorry for everything, and she began to cry.

She heard a little cough and looked up. Mr Wood was smiling at her and her teacher was with him.

'I think Mr Wood can explain everything to you much better than I can, Jessie.' She went very quietly to her desk to do some marking.

Mr Wood sat down near Jessie.

'Don't worry, Lass,' he said in the kindest, gentlest voice. 'You see, these seeds that have bolted off, they're a bit leggy and there is a chance they may bend and snap and then there will be no flower. Yours are taking it slowly. They'll probably be shorter but sturdier, when they do came through. They are usually the strongest plants. 'Slow and steady wins the race'. Do you know the story of the Hare and the Tortoise?'

Jessie nodded.

'You just keep telling the little seeds how good they are and they'll be through in no time.' Jessie dried her eyes and looked carefully at her pot.

The next day, she couldn't believe her eyes! She was sure she could see a small, round green leaflet trying to break through.

'Come on,' she said. 'Come on – you can do it.' And by home time it had! Sam was first out of the compost and Jessie couldn't wait to get home and tell her Dad.

'There we go again, though,' she thought, 'waiting is such a tough thing to do, but I think I am getting better at it, especially when the wait is worth it, like waiting for these seeds!'

Follow-up questions

- What made Jessie think that she had killed all her seeds?
- Why did Jessie think that being patient and waiting were so very hard to do?

Tell no Lies

Theme: Harvest and the giant combines bring fear to the Forest and in the dead, black night the food chain manifests itself. Top-of-the-food-chain Fox takes advantage of the dark night whilst everyone is not being as vigilant as they normally would be.

Setting: In the forest

Curriculum reference: Science (food-chains)

As the Sun sank below the horizon and the pale Moon took her turn to light the sky, different creatures began to stir in the forest.

Owl hooted softly and waited to see if another owl would hoot back.

Field Mouse scurried about here and there, rustling the dry Autumn leaves, as she searched for good seeds to bury for the Winter months ahead.

Dog Fox barked at the moon. He liked the black night; it meant that Farmer James was asleep and wouldn't see him, streaking across the fields to the hen-house.

Roe Deer stamped her delicate hoof to bring her little fawn back by her side. She had found a good place to lie and keep watch.

Hedgehog uncurled slowly and stretched a mighty stretch, before trotting at quite a pace towards Mr Heath's garden, where she knew he would have left out a supper for her.

Everything in the woodland was as it should be.

Suddenly dozy Dormouse, who was usually so quiet, came helter-skelter through the forest. He was bowling along like a tiny ball. He was running so quickly that his feet couldn't stay in touch with the ground.

He squeaked and squawked and generally drew attention to himself in an alarming way, so that all the creatures took notice. This was something he didn't usually do!

Every creature stood as still as a statue and waited! Not one creature breathed, in or out! They could all hear the noise in the distance. They sensed its path as it got nearer and nearer.

None of the creatures were truly afraid though. They thought the danger was a long way off. They recognized the tiny warning noises of Dormouse, but they didn't realize there was more imminent danger than even the Dormouse knew.

'Oh, my whiskers!' called Dormouse. 'Oh my goodness!' He rolled down the bank. 'It's coming, it's coming and it's so bright I couldn't see what it is!' he squeaked.

Owl swooped silently down. Field Mouse scurried towards her friend.

'What is it, Dormouse?' they asked. 'What has frightened you so badly?'

'It's, it's, it's a –' panted the tiny creature.

'What?' they asked.

Dormouse breathed in a huge breath and gasped out the words, 'It's a spaceship!'

'A spaceship?' hooted Owl. 'What tosh!'

'Utter nonsense,' said sensible Field Mouse.

'Phrumph!' snuffed Hedgehog.

'Really, and they're coming across the fields to get us,' whispered Dormouse, his voice so faint they had to lean close to hear him.

Owl took charge. 'I shall fly over the woodland and take a 'recci' as they say.' And with that he was gone. All the creatures waited. And waited.

Field Mouse got agitated rather more quickly than the rest. 'Dormouse, are you sure? We all know you are a daft, dozy dormouse. Have you made this up?'

Dormouse looked affronted. 'No!' he squeaked.

'If you are telling lies, Dormouse – I shall eat you for my supper!' said sly Dog Fox, who had crept up when none of them were looking. His tummy was rumbling.

'Oh no, you won't!' wheezed Dormouse. 'I saw it with my own eyes.'

Roe Deer whimpered and her huge eyes grew even wider as she feared for her fawn.

'Listen,' said Hedgehog, 'if this is a hoax, Dormouse, it's not a safe one. With all your noise, you have managed to bring together far too many enemies.

There's a whole food-chain here and I for one am not feeling happy about it,' she grumbled.

'Honest, it is true,' said Dormouse. 'I promise I saw a huge, blinding light. I did! I did!'

Slowly, one by one, each frightened animal sloped off quietly to hide. They were afraid to stay and they wanted to be far away from sly Dog Fox!

Consequently when Owl did return there was no one there.

Owl spoke loudly, he knew all the other creatures were hiding nearby, away from Mr Top-of-the-food-chain Dog Fox.

'I'm afraid Dormouse was both right and wrong,' Owl intoned.

'The big lights he saw were in fact the headlights of the huge combine harvesters gathering to cut the corn and the grass meadows. Tomorrow night our world will look like a different planet. All will be flat, cut down, no food, no places to hide. Indeed it will be as if aliens had landed and devastated our world and our lives.'

He paused for all this to sink in and then added gravely.

'You must go and warn your families and all the other creatures. They need to move quickly from the fields or they will be killed.'

The rest of the animals moved on. But not Dormouse…

Dog Fox smiled. He licked his lips. After a tasty little Dormouse snack, he was heading for the hen-house.

Follow-up questions

- Can you think how Dormouse could have passed on her warning without causing such a disturbance?

- Can you describe the food web of creatures mentioned in this story?

Lightning Source UK Ltd.
Milton Keynes UK
UKOW04f0144060217

293696UK00006B/58/P